The Zen of Crisis

by Michelle Robinson

Published by:

FriesenPress

Suite 300 – 852 Fort Street
Victoria, BC, Canada V8W 1H8

www.friesenpress.com

Distributed to the trade by The Ingram Book Company

Table of Contents

To

Daniel,
Sierra
&
Easton

Such beautiful spirits.

~You are my inspiration~

Acknowledgements

This book has spilled tumultuously from my mind, in messy drips and pools. The beliefs and truths I share were nurtured through my experiences and I am indebted to my incredible mom and dad who, despite our occasional differences, have taught me the value of love, understanding, generosity and following your heart. I love you both dearly.

None of this could have been possible without the efforts and professionalism of the entire medical staff at Vancouver Children's Hospital, who were intricately involved in the fight for Sierra's survival, as well as Dr. Penney, and the pediatric team at Kelowna General Hospital.

Thank you to my sister Tamara Hodge, your laughter and smile have been a lifeline so many times. The ongoing encouragement and support of our extended family has been critical. Special gratitude to Lillian and Harvey Robinson for all of their love and support as well as that of Dennis Baxendale, Jo Scott, Aspen, Cindy and Dan Puklicz, Linda and Don Barry, Shannon, Christopher, Michelle, Wade and Wyatt, Greg and the entire Poy clan, Hermida and Ralph Smith, Jen and Rob Hopkinson and Terry, Norval Bradley and Ted Callahan. We are also indebted to Jen Stamp and Tara Hedrich, June Brownrigg, Jen and Hugh Bitz, Josie and Rick Salel, Jeanette White, Shannon and Alan Marjoribanks, Jen and Hal Spelliscy, Cory and Al Tout, Peter Henry and Maureen Valley. You are all so dear to our hearts.

Inspiration and editing has come in many waves from Naomi Erickson, Joan Allen, Lana O'Brien, Judy Arden, Colleen Knox, Tara Hedrich, Charmalee Kirk, and Carole Poy. Your guidance and reflections have inspired me beyond words.

Special thanks to Ailsa Edge who, through sad circumstance, proved to me that I have a voice and was the catalyst which spurred my awkward creativity. I would also like to thank Sherida and Steve Peters for their amazing strength.

To my children, I am in awe of your courage and thank you for your patience during this process. You are the very essence of purity... stay that way!

Finally, I express my appreciation and gratitude to my husband, Mark Robinson, who I see through so many different lenses. Thank you for allowing me to express my deepest nature and encouraging me to be who I have become. The road has not always been pretty, but you have been steadfast and unwavering in your dedication to me despite it all.

This is a true story, but some of the names of characters have been changed to protect the identities of those involved. The following is my recollection of the events as I remember them. Both hospitals and all of the medical staff were impeccable with the level of care and attention they provided and we are deeply indebted to all of the physicians, nurses and support staff involved.

When you examine the lives of the most influential people who have ever walked among us, you discover one thread that winds through them all; they have all been aligned first to their spiritual nature and only then to their physical selves.

~ Albert Einstein

Prologue

This writing has two levels. You may read it as a story, to follow the miraculous journey Sierra takes, or choose to look deeper at the fundamental lessons that have brought me great peace and insight. While I would do anything to take away the pain and torment my child and family went through, I am thankful for the experience and do not wish it away. The growth and level of consciousness I discovered through this ordeal have been life changing and I hope the words will ring true to those who can feel the "oneness" I stumbled upon.

I am in no way "enlightened", rather, very far from it, but enough happened to allow me regular glimpses into an amazing world for which I am grateful and this is my endeavor to share these moments with others. Given the choice, I would experience it all again, no matter how painful, as it was the only way for me to overcome ingrained selfishness and narrow mindedness that is so rampant in our society today.

The pictures of Sierra's beginning have been included, not to shock, but rather to show that the unbelievable is possible, and to reinforce that by the cooperation and true belief of many, the impossible can occur.

I wish one day, we all could experience a true level of selflessness and see this global community for just that; one intricate entity, so deeply entwined in all that is. The step is so simple it is deceptive. The difficulty lies in the level of trust required and in the choice to relinquish control, a control which in the end is false and is the debilitating factor in us all as a race.

~ Michelle Robinson

Human beings,
vegetables or cosmic dust,
we all dance to a
mysterious tune,
intoned in the distance
by an invisible player.

~ Albert Einstein

Chapter 1

Her fragile body lay tangled beneath the twisting, life giving maze. If moments can be crystallized, this remains forever embedded in my mind; time frozen in a florescent lie. Nurses and doctors clamoring for access around her tiny newborn frame, speaking in tongue too rapid to comprehend. My soul, for an instant, forever suspended with hers in a false paralytic state.

Three hours before I had been methodically sliced open to retrieve her, teams of nurses and neonatologists at the ready. Although they tried their best to distract, I heard her first pathetic gurgles as she gasped in vain, her body betraying her in its very first attempt at life. They didn't show her to me.

An anesthetic haze overtakes the minutes that immediately followed. Some days I am grateful for those moments; a blurry pillow of confusion to smother the haunting images.

A Polaroid was my first glimpse of Sierra, permeated by a cyanotic shade. Irony spat its ugly grin through her perfect baby form. Ten fingers, ten toes, smooth silky skin, a tuft of dark black hair, but artificially limp limbs betrayed the classic baby photo.

Nothing could prepare a parent. There are no words for those first moments. Gradually, some sense assembles; one monitor for oxygen, one for her heart, countless tubes emitting haphazardly, wherever a line could take. Doctors hover anxiously, averting their gaze in apologetic shame. Finally, a familiar physician takes us aside. "Assessments have suggested… stats are leading to… moderate severity." Diaphragmatic hernia has become an all consuming sentence, its physiology firmly implanted in our minds.

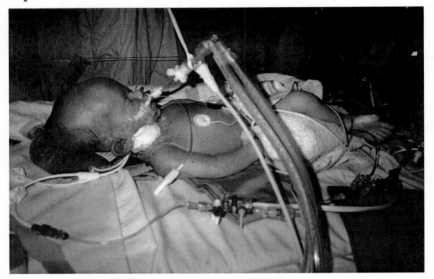

Sierra: 3½ hours old.

Day 1

I had been glued to Sierra's side from the moment they allowed me to leave the post operating observation room. I was still under some effect of the anesthetic from the cesarean, but I wouldn't leave her. Mark stayed until he was satisfied she was stable then he went to check on our son, Daniel.

I remember the harsh light of the florescent bulbs, illuminating every painful truth. Her body was beautiful, round and plump, a little roll of fat over each elbow, but thin white tape crisscrossed in a maze over her mouth, holding the ventilator in place. Tubes, which at the time befuddled me, snaked across her newborn skin.

She had been paralyzed and sedated in order to be on the ventilator and now she lay eerily motionless on the sheets. We knew this would happen, but the theory the doctors had confidently shared didn't begin to prepare us for the harsh reality we now witnessed.

A young respiratory technician tracked her CO_2 levels on a paper wall chart behind me. I interrupted him once quietly to ask what it was for. Now I realize he was basically keeping track of the poison which was threatening to kill my daughter. I glanced periodically in his direction, while I stroked a patch of the skin on Sierra's arm that was bereft of plastic tubing. My hand froze. The technician had been making pencil marks every ten minutes. Now the marks were spiking; hugely. I turned away and looked bewildered at the heart monitor. At this point, I had little idea of what heart rate was reasonable considering her condition, but the numbers climbed at an alarming rate. Activity around me began to swirl and I gripped tightly to the arms of the wheel chair, hoping to steady myself in the center of the tornado.

To my disbelief, the technician began to make marks off the chart onto the wall itself, his relay of messages to the nurse increasing in speed and intensity. Her CO_2 levels were climbing so high there weren't high enough intervals on the sheet to chart the rise.

Later we were told that Sierra's only functioning lung collapsed, blood vessels rupturing. All tracking of time gets distorted in the hospital. The florescent sun burns regardless twenty four hours. Nurses and doctors functioned around Sierra and I, not asking me to leave, as if they knew we were one entity. Flurries of activity and discussions swirled in funnels around us, as I stared longingly at my daughter, watching each mechanical breath raise her tiny chest. Numbers which then meant little to me flickered dramatically on the screens; red, blue and green neon prisms dancing round the room. The severity of Sierra's condition was no longer being masked. I was in the midst of the medical fury; serious, intent looks deeply etched on the faces of those around me.

Twelve doctors and nurses began to rush into the room and I knew it was time I call Mark back to the hospital. I wheeled out backwards in disbelief to let the army of practitioners do their job.

Mark arrived within 15 minutes. The neonatal unit was in flux. The head neonatologist motioned us aside and very calmly looked in our eyes. He held a piece of paper that dangled in waiting. To this day I don't know where those doctors get their courage. I opened my hands to hold it, trying to steady it as they shook. I began to read. Words jumped jarringly from the page; brain damage, high risk of mortality, uncontrolled bleeding in the brain. My tears created a sea so thick I could no longer see. I passed the sheet in vain to Mark. It was Mark who had the strength to hold the pen and sign his consent on the form to put Sierra on the life saving machine.

I cried uncontrollably in the room for a few minutes, watching as more and more medical staff flooded into the area. I was now outside her isolated room, in the general special care unit where other parents hovered closely near their sick or premature infants. When it got to the point I could no longer see Sierra for bodies two deep, I asked Mark to take me up to my room. I could no longer reach my daughter and she lay dying. I had to leave the area to make room for those who had any chance of saving my baby girl.

Mark wheeled me down the long twisting corridors, while my soul folded in on itself again and again like some complex origami. I shut my eyes as tightly as I could.

Suddenly, I heard a primitive wail from down the hall. It shocked me into looking up. My eyes fought to focus through the saline blur, but I saw no one. Mark and I were alone in this hallway. Who had screamed? It took seconds, but then it registered. That primeval scream had burst from my chest, bubbled up through my vice clamped throat and exploded from my lips. I was screaming a death cry for my daughter.

At 1 am, Dr. Solimano entered my room. I had yet to sleep; grief and adrenaline coursed through every cell in my body. He moved slowly to the side of the room and pulled a metal chair up to my bed. I repositioned, bracing to hear the news he held.

He began with, "The operation on to ECMO went well." A lengthy explanation followed, but I was too busy rejoicing at the fact that she was still in this realm. Dim light illuminated his frame as he spoke. They had placed her onto a system of machinery that replaced her pulmonary system, diverting the blood from her heart straight through a machine that oxygenated her blood then led it back to her heart to be pumped to the rest of her body. Her lung was badly damaged and they were accessing her continuously.

As Dr. Solimano concluded, my muscles relaxed enough for my jaw to mouth a thank you. He smiled, but I saw moisture in his tired gaze. He excused himself to go back to her side and I collapsed against the blankets, praying for Sierra to be strong.

Day 3

I had wheeled myself down to the ICU, been buzzed in and sterilized my still supple skin. I was getting more adept at moving the wheel chair and my operation site on my abdomen was beginning to heal. I circled around past the nursing station, wheeling towards Sierra's *embryonic cocoon*.

Two dear friends had the courage and insight to put their family's life on hold and come down to Vancouver to be with us that first week. Coming in to the ICU to visit, they miraculously kept the horror from their faces, however, they couldn't mask a brief hesitation in their step before entering the fully glassed in room. A tiny body lay central beneath a labyrinth of tubes and sensors monitored by multiple machines and pumps. My friend's husband, so true to his nature, swooped curiously around to get a read on each machine, assessing whether it would suffice.

Sierra had a plastic dome over her head, which was craned to one side. The canula from the ECMO machine was inserted into her neck in the carotid artery. During surgery, crimson blood had trickled from the insertion site of the central line down her neck, and now it was preserved by a clear plastic bandage holding down wads of gauze. IV needles were inserted in her cranium, now shaved to accommodate the lines. Other intravenous needles were bound to both hands and tiny feet, colour coded clamps to track which medications each delivered. A tube had been inserted through her nose into her stomach to drain the vile and more caked blood was pasted on her scalp, creating a cracked, intricate pattern.

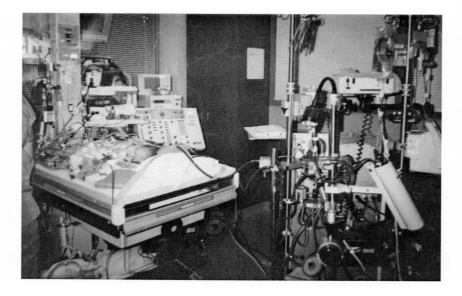

Sierra on ECMO: Extra-Corporeal Membrane Oxygenation.

By day three, a familiarity was settling over me. I would reach out and stroke my child's skin, gently allowing my fingers to brush over the dried blood above her ear that could not yet be sponged off due to the delicate, precarious position of the life saving canula. I was no longer afraid of the machines which anchored my daughter to this world. I would watch her bodily fluids drain through tubes, air bubbles being gently led away.

A nurse and technician were with her twenty four hours a day, monitoring every stat imaginable. Blood was drawn every few hours to monitor her blood gas levels. I was soon told Sierra was getting these tests processed so quickly because she was the most critical pediatric case in B.C. at the time.

I had quietly asked a fraction of the questions that swirled in confusion in my head. I knew what some of the monitors were tracking. I knew some of the key parameters her stats could hover between.

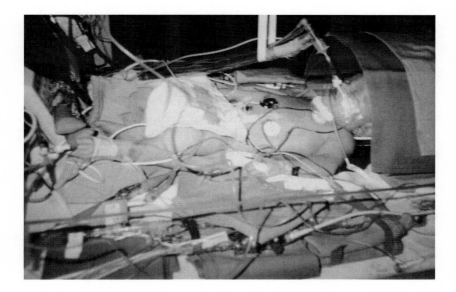

The nurses moved with precision and patiently explained the purpose of each medication. The banter between the doctors, nurses and technicians was still 90% unknown to me, but I listened with the intent of a toddler, trying to grasp every familiar root word and medical term fleeting frantically through the air. It was as if, along with Sierra, I had been abruptly reborn into a foreign world and now had to get my bearings.

I was asked to move for a few minutes as they wheeled in the portable cardio-echogram machine. This I recognized from the monthly visits to the Women's Hospital to monitor Sierra's development, only instead of the icy cold gel being smeared on my belly, it was now gently rubbed on her chest and the secrets of her heart were revealed.

They completed the test, then, moments later, the large machine to scan her brain was wheeled in. The medical team was looking for any signs of bleeding on the brain, which was of high risk because of the strong blood thinners Sierra was on to prevent clotting on the ECMO machine. All the blood from her body was being re-routed through the canula to the ECMO machine.

ECMO stands for exo-corporeal membrane oxygenation, which meant instead of her lungs oxygenating her blood, they were being completely bypassed and the machine was oxygenating it for her. The idea was that each day on the ECMO machine would buy her lungs time to recover. The canula led her bright red blood through a dizzying array of clear tubes feeding into the machine. An ECMO technician sat at the machine twenty four hours a day, monitoring the flow of oxygen back in to my daughter's heart. He was a diligent man who tried hard to maintain some lighthearted, upbeat conversation despite the horrific circumstances. We were soon told Sierra had two ventricular septal defects. That is "doctor" for two holes in her heart. The holes were situated low in the muscle tissue separating the two ventrical chambers of the heart. Essentially, blood that had yet to be oxygenated was flowing through these holes back into her system, further robbing her cells of critical oxygen.

Dr. Solimano entered and I asked a few more questions based on the research I had done and the memorization of terms I had crammed in the days before her birth. His eyes scrunched as he listened to me tackle the Latin, then, he motioned for me to come see something. I was confused, because he began walking away from Sierra's pressurized room. I awkwardly wheeled myself after him, and we circled around to a small, dark room with a lit up screen. Comprehension dawned. Glowing on the backlit wall, I realized we were looking at Sierra's X rays taken earlier that day. He asked me to come closer so he could explain to me.

He pointed to a dark area on the screen. His smooth skin reflected the muted, eerie light. "This is Sierra's right lung. It is the one that collapsed the first night. We are watching closely to see if the damage is beginning to repair, and the good news is some gains are being made."

Balance ... always in life. If there is good news mentioned, it means the bad is soon to follow.

He continued. "This dark spot," he moved his fingers to a tiny dot. "This is Sierra's left lung. She only has 5 percent of left lung tissue."

The question we had all been asking... what exactly are we dealing with. Now, with blinding clarity, we knew.

I flashed back to months before. Sierra's birth defect had first been picked up by the 18 week routine ultrasound. The excitement I had about getting a glimpse of my unborn fetus gradually waned as the ultrasound technician excused herself part way through the exam and said she needed to check on something and get the photos. I lay there in blissful ignorance, looking at the pictures around the room silently questioning the designer's choice in wall colour. Absentmindedly, I stroked my belly where the cold gel had made me itchy. Little jabs poked, eliciting a warm smile on my lips. Minutes and minutes went by. How did I not realize something was amiss? Fortunately, I was lost in my thoughts, thinking the woman would soon come back with the take home snapshots of my daughter.

Now, sitting staring at the X-ray with Dr. Solimano, it was becoming heart wrenchingly clear. He continued to explain that the hole in Sierra's diaphragm had allowed many abdominal organs to rise up into the chest cavity. Besides helping to inflate the lungs, a properly developed diaphragm acts as a barrier, separating the two areas. The hole in Sierra's diaphragm had been large enough to let the left lobe of the liver rise into the chest, as well as the stomach, spleen and part of the small intestines. This in turn had impeded proper development of the lungs and heart in the crowded chest cavity. The left lung had been hardest hit because it was directly above the entrance and the abdominal organs had squished it into near oblivion. Hence, we stood staring at the five percent dark spot of tissue on the screen.

Sierra had further complications. By now, this did not surprise me. A calm resignation had begun to take me over, which in hindsight was self-preservation at work. Dr. Solimano explained that Sierra had a condition called PPNH or Persistent Pulmonary Neonatal Hypertension.

"It is particularly dangerous because in infants with Sierra's condition, the pulmonary vascular veins are more muscular than a normal infant."

I got excited the first time I had read this, thinking "more muscular" meant stronger, which would be a bonus in her favour. However, upon further reading, I realized it was one of the cruelest tricks of nature. This birth defect causes an increased closing of the blood vessels when experiencing stress, which is high blood pressure, but for these poor children, the vessels just don't narrow, they can completely squeeze shut! This was why Sierra's blood vessels burst the very first night and led to the collapse of her right lung, the only full size lung she had.

I explained what I knew of this, using the technical terms to converse with Dr. Solimano and his eyes lit up.

"You are very smart." He looked intensely at me. If only he knew the truth.

"I read a lot about this before she was born." I said meekly, not explaining I had researched it with a frightening fervor as her birth approached. We had been told Sierra, at best, only had a 25% chance of survival. Those lonely, silent evenings in the weeks leading up to Sierra's birth almost destroyed me. I found the only way I could turn off my fear was to go swim countless laps despite the drag of my belly or go on line to read medical journals and learn everything I could about the physiology of the disabling condition cursing my daughter. I would stay up into the wee hours reading indecipherable medical reports. The text was so complex, I had to refer to the medical glossary every three or four words to get a basic understanding. I wrote out pages and pages of terminology and studied it, so I could formulate knowledgeable questions and have some idea of what the doctors were saying.

I now looked back at Dr. Solimano, hoping he would never realize how my medical knowledge seeking was the only thin string that held me together those final weeks. He continued looking at me, then proceeded with his explanation of some procedures they were hoping to try. He didn't dumb down the language for me, and I understood many of the Latin medical terms he used. I asked him questions stemming from the research and he answered them, fully bringing me in to the rationale behind his decisions.

When I returned to Sierra's cocoon, the hum of the machines wrapped me in a now familiar warmth. I said a quiet hello to Jenna, her nurse, then began singing to Sierra in a shy, soft voice while the nurse recorded reams of details on the charts. I sang Jamaican calypsos, songs my mom had sang, wishing I had half her singing voice. I reached over to hold the strange voodoo looking doll the current nurse had given her. I looked up at Jenna now, her strong arms repositioning Sierra so bed sores wouldn't develop. Jenna's beautiful black skin shone in the light on the heart monitor as she moved to Sierra's feet to adjust a clamp on a tube. She saw me holding the strange doll made from scraps of material with corn-rowed hair. The doll looked like a miniature Jenna.

She smiled broadly, "I got that from one of the crafters in the foyer earlier today. Isn't it cute? I thought it would bring Sierra luck."

I smiled back as I thumbed the bizarre looking caricature. Jenna then reached down into a bag and handed something else to me. I reached up to take hold of a blanket and she began her explanation.

"The nurses in the Special Care Nursery wanted me to give it to you."

I unfolded the material, seeing dainty pink, blue and yellow squares sewn into a quilt. I looked up in confusion.

"It's a quilt that some of the volunteers make for the families here." She was quiet, and then added, "They give it to parents whose children may not make it."

My heart froze in my chest. I wanted to reach across and attack this woman for letting those words loose in this room. How could she say that to my face, after sharing countless hours with me, caring diligently for my child?

I continued to stare at her, holding the quilt as if it carried the plague.

She continued on with her duties, writing down more data on the chart. The hum became deafening and tears welled up in my eyes. I slowly realized, Jenna wasn't trying to be cruel… she was attempting to prepare me for a moment I refused to consider.

I wheeled away angrily with the blanket and found the storage room where I had been allowed to awkwardly pump breast milk. Every three to four hours I attached myself to a metal beast that suctioned the life giving formula from my breasts. The pain, guilt and confusion associated with that machine cannot be explained. There is no warm, snuggly baby to position at your chest, no cooing sounds to offset the painful stab as the milk gets drawn down. There is only sterile tubing and hard white vials to be filed, labeled and stored in waiting in a hospital fridge. The saddest part was placing my bottled milk in beside all the other bottled milk drawn from countless other mothers who were living a similar nightmare.

This pumping break, I wedged myself far into the storage area to gain more privacy, and stewed in my anger at the thoughtless words that had been said. I glared at the blanket in my hands, meant to be a thoughtful gift. I put it down eventually and looked around for something to take my mind off the scathing words and hard pull of the pump, when I glanced at the oddest thing. A storage container was partially opened and read "foot mold". At first, I thought that it was something to stop foot mold, but before I could glance away, I found the truth. A tiny plaster foot had been created and was labeled with a date of birth and date of death. I think I stopped breathing. I was enclosed in a room with other parents' final treasures, impressions from children who had moved on.

I ended the pumping session quickly and coiled the tubing before making my way back to Sierra. I rolled in beside her and resumed my vigil, the hum engulfing me again.

Several hours later, the strangest moment in my life occurred.

Sierra began to take a rapid turn for the worse. Unscheduled consultations and testing began to gain speed around me. Physicians began appearing at a dizzying rate and I repeatedly repositioned to allow them room to function. Doctors and technicians moved into the language too quickly to follow, but I only needed to listen to tone and inflection to know an emergency had evolved.

At one point, they began to draw blood from Sierra every half hour, and transfusions were given to replace her platelet levels. The confusion and urgency became too much and I realized I could no longer fake this stoic pose. I decided to flee the ICU before it destroyed what was left of me. I began to wheel frantically down the wing, past the nursing station, my inner voice was screaming to escape. Suddenly, a small clear voice broke through the chaos in my mind. I froze in my tracks as it spoke.

"Don't give up on me."

I sat stunned and stopped wheeling the chair. Five short words, spoken in the voice of a five year old echoed loudly in my head. In a heartbeat I knew it was Sierra. She was calling to me in a way I may never comprehend, and I felt a strong presence of my grandfather. I was motionless, suspended in a moment I could not explain, but fully understood. If there was ever a moment in my life when I could have truly gone mad, that was it, but instead, it was at that moment I chose to finally bond with my daughter. She needed me more than ever and in some way, my presence was giving her strength. I realized in that instant that no matter how badly it hurt to sit and watch what was happening to her, I was her mother and she needed me there, no matter what.

I breathed deeply and slowly turned the chair around, once again rejoining the chaotic flurry surrounding her, but this time with a strong, calm resolve, not flinching any longer at the horror, just focusing on the little being in the crux of it all.

To the mind that is still,
the whole universe surrenders.

~ Loa Tzu

Chapter 2

Mark and I laughed as we spun around, random scratches further etched on the community center floor. The reception was a relaxed, joyful affair, with music loudly pulsing through the hall. "Fishing in the Dark" echoed boisterously as I jostled my now bulging frame across the floor.

Earlier that afternoon, our friends' wedding had been delayed due to the late arrival of the photographer; this gave guests the rare time to mingle in the hot church pews. The bride was lovely when she did finally walk through, to the relief of everyone. Now at the reception, friends sat joking, the bride and groom cut the sloping cake and giggled across the room. There are times when one senses things are too good to last.

The following morning the call came. Sunlight gently filtered through our window, but it hung grey and musty on my skin. The pediatrician's words clamored over and over in my mind.

I immediately called Mark to let him know we should both be at the meeting. I could tell from the doctor's voice that the news was somewhat serious. The first time we met the obstetrician, a pregnancy before, I sat cold and rigid in emergency, waiting for Mark to arrive. I had been there for three hours, by then realizing I had most likely lost the baby.

The doctor, looking so young, walked in calmly soon after Mark arrived. Her body belied her exhaustion, as she leant heavily against the beige concrete wall. She said that after reviewing the ultrasound it revealed more than just losing a baby. She believed there were two embryos, one now washed away, the other lodged at the base of my fallopian tube, growing snuggly into the tissue of my uterine wall.

Elation washed over me for a moment as I thought this other "twin" might have a chance. But the explanation continued.

This was a "corneal ectopic" pregnancy; her words staccatoed playfully off the concrete walls. She quietly explained that the baby's tissue was growing into my tissue. The fallopian tube and uterine wall would soon burst, causing internal bleeding, putting my life in danger.

Pain can increase exponentially. Now this embryo was a potential life threatening growth. But there was more. The ultrasound also revealed growths on my ovaries, so when they did operate within the next hour, there was the real possibility that they may find cancerous lumps, and need to remove not only my fallopian tube, but the ovary as well.

The mind does strange things for protection. I grew very still, focusing on the rhythmic sound of her words. They prepared me for the emergency surgery. Mark didn't want to stay. I gazed through him in disbelief. He has a hard time accepting physical weakness, as if this was my fault. He wanted to go to get our son from our neighbours and tuck him into bed. Resentment that may never dissolve welled up in my eyes. I begged for him to stay at least until I came out of the operation. He finally conceded, but it is a truth I will never forget.

In a haze, I opened my eyes now in the patient ward. In disbelief, I soon realized it was the maternity ward. Faint cries of new life echoed in the distance. The doctor, very empathetically, explained that they had removed the fallopian tube with the embryo and had to take a "chunk" of the uterine wall. She drew a picture, more of a snake, than a woman's reproductive organs, showing me where the "baby" had been and how large it had become. She explained how close I had come to my uterus erupting into my internal organs, and how big a piece of the uterine wall had been carved away. I had a chance of carrying another baby, as the uterine muscle which remained was very thin, but that I would never be able to go through a natural labour, because contractions would rupture the uterus at that point. She explained that they were able to save the ovary as only benign lumps were found. The doctor politely said her regrets. I politely said a mere thank you for saving me, and sank hard against the plastic pillow.

Now, a year later, we sat once again in her medical office, watching her greet us with pure professionalism, ensuring we were comfortable before listening to the news ahead. Her calm demeanor floundered for a moment, as she averted her eyes, took a deep breath and fidgeted with the edge of the file. An icy rigidness flowed over me as my body braced for the news ahead.

"I reviewed your ultrasound."

A familiar vice clenched my chest.

"The baby is growing well, but...", it hung suspended in the air, "the diaphragm has not formed properly. There is a hole in the tissue, and the baby's abdominal organs have moved into the chest cavity."

I can't remember if I glanced at Mark. My muscles were so tight and rigid I don't imagine I took my eyes off the file in her hands.

The doctor continued, "Children born with this defect have a good chance of survival. The fetus will need to be monitored closely throughout the pregnancy, and an operation will be performed once the baby is born."

That initial explanation didn't begin to scratch the mere surface of the battle and trauma that lay ahead for our little girl. This incredibly talented and compassionate physician could never have guessed how disastrous the diagnosis would prove to be.

I do remember getting in the car with Mark. We slowly walked in silence through the open parking lot. He may have opened the door for me. Mark hovered like a male quail with its mate, tentative and skitterish at the slightest flutter.

Again, I grew calm and silent, trying to focus on the positive shreds of information the physician had provided.

This moment proved to be the end of my blissful world with my nearly three year old son. Physicians relay facts and always too many percentages and statistics. They fail to tell you how embracing a challenge associated with physical diseases or birth defects will radically and often tragically affect every dynamic of every relationship in one's life. Hindsight has allowed me to see both the damage our family endured and the treasured moments and insights we have taken away.

Life is unpredictable, but I wish we had had a better glimpse of the iceberg we were about to crash into headlong.

A sharp, jagged edge
Carves away at my soul
Scathing, removing, reshaping
Succulent drops of hope fall from my cheeks.
Strong feet jab unknowingly in my womb
Growing silently, assuredly.
In six revolutions you will be here
To battle a foreign world
My protection to no longer suffice
Independent, your singing soul will dwell
Among us
You seem stronger in faith than I
Trusting and being
Silent, strong daughter
I am already proud of you.

Chapter 3

Day 4

In the constant ebb and flow of life, there are plateaus. It is an essential factor in the cycle of all existence, but the most frightening plateau is just before the soul moves on to its next form. Energy is never lost, it only alters state, but to be so close to this metamorphosis … our minds continued to struggle.

Dr. Solimano and Dr. Singh had been on constant vigils following each dizzying shred of evidence, watching as Sierra's status changed hourly. The gains her lung had made the first few days were promising, but now, progress halted.

A team of 56 physicians, specialists and technicians began a heated debate as to whether her diaphragmatic hernia operation should be performed while she was still on ECMO. The operation would involve moving the stomach, spleen, liver and small intestines back down into the abdominal area, opening up her chest cavity to allow the lung and heart their rightful space. The displaced left lobe of the liver was of greatest concern because the many blood vessels supplying it could easily be kinked during repositioning, cutting off blood to the organ. Dr. Schenkle had successfully completed one operation like this while at Stanford, but it had never been attempted at Children's Hospital.

I silently sat at the side as I witnessed a large group gathered outside Sierra's glassed in area. I remember the intense dialogue rallied back and forth as each individual of the team countered with their rationale, for or against. I can't pretend to know what each issue was, but one very real element was the blood thinners. In order to prevent the blood from clotting in the tubing of the ECMO machine, high doses of the medicine had been essential, but this also increased the likelihood of Sierra bleeding to death during an operation while on this technology. The crowd dispersed to consult further experts via email. Finally, after great debate, it was decided that the benefits outweighed the risks and the team chose to move forward with the operation.

An hour later, activity heightened as Sierra was being prepped for surgery. Movement increased around her tiny space as specialists prepared for a multitude of eventualities. Blood for further transfusions lay guarded in waiting. Specialized nurses prepped Sierra as a palpable weight of concern settled heavily in her room. Eventually, by some act of grace, someone had the foresight to cancel the procedure at the last moment.

Mark and I were overcome with relief, but the speculation as to what would happen next became a crushing weight on everyone involved.

Sierra continued to hover on this precarious precipice for three more days, and then, as each collective nerve had reached breaking point, the next move presented itself with unrelenting clarity.

Day 7

While those in a coma can be kept alive by ventilators and cardiac apparatus, the human body cannot be indefinitely supported by the ECMO technology. A maximum of 7– 10 days is all that can be endured before the severe, imperfect mechanical pressures of technology have their detrimental and final effects on the delicate body tissues. We had reached day 7 and Dr. Solimano and Dr. Singh silently ushered Mark and I away from the flashing machines, out of the ICU and into a small consultation room.

The lighting was hushed. A beige dial phone sat patiently waiting on a side table littered with magazines previously quenched with the tears of many.

Very calmly, the doctors delivered the news, like two parents divulging the truth about Santa. They slowly explained that the canula going into the carotid artery was damaging the blood vessel so badly, the only option was to remove the canula and embed it directly into the right atrium of Sierra's heart. Again, they would have to slice into this poor little being, who had endured so much, just to keep her on life support. The right lung tissue had not made further progress in repairing itself, and most likely, had reached its pinnacle of function.

Mark and I looked at each other and spoke scattered reasoning out loud in the doctors' presence.

We both felt Sierra had been through enough. We both believed it would be for purely selfish reasons to pursue keeping her on life support. We both agreed she needed to be set free.

It was the ultimate test of selfless love.

The doctors commended us on our decision, fully prepared to do whatever we had wished, but the definitive truth enveloped us all in the tiny room.

I don't remember the moments that immediately followed. Our bodies and minds had been on red alert for so long, any concept of time or normalcy had been wildly distorted. We may have sat there together ... I do remember a scrunched tissue in hand. The tunnel vision skewed any perception of others. We must have gone back to be with her, but it became a calm silence of waiting. At best, we were numb.

Sierra was prepped for the operation to be removed from the ECMO machine and back to a regular ventilator to wait out the final hours. That waiting room became a cocoon as we delicately contoured to the pressure of time's hand. Neither Mark nor I had any clue as to what creatures would emerge.

The operation was two hours. Finally, a weary Dr. Solimano and Dr. Singh returned saying Sierra was now off the life support of ECMO and only on a ventilator. All that was left to do was wait.

Six days before I gave birth to Sierra, I had a dream. I was well aware that the cesarean was coming up, and in the dream I was in the operating room surrounded by nurses and physicians.

Doctors reached in to get Sierra and out she came, singing.

After being removed from ECMO, Sierra's oxygen needs remained extremely high on the ventilator. Normal room oxygen which we all need to survive is 21%. Sierra was being supplemented with over 50% oxygen concentration and this fluttered up and down in chaotic disarray. She still remained in the ICU, but the ECMO team, exhausted from the week long ordeal, was being reassembled as a new child faced the possibility of needing the intervention.

The day after Sierra was taken off ECMO, the head of the team asked if I felt comfortable speaking to the mother of a new child who was in need of the machine. In a span of 7 days, my interpretation of the technology had changed from that of inconceivable horror to that of comforting awe as it seemed a natural extension of my child's existence. I had spent hours watching her beautiful scarlet blood stream steadily through the spooling cylindrical tubing. I had watched as plastic bags of plasma swung suspended off the IV poles. The scrambled mass of IV lines now had a familiarity, a known purpose and my fear had melted into appreciation and quiet calm.

That was not what was reflected in this new woman's eyes as she approached our room with her mother. I clearly saw the repulsion and terror as her focus darted sporadically from one monitor to the next and I recognized her need to flee this reality as I had tried days before. I used a calm voice and attempted to explain how amazing each piece of technology was, how it had aided my daughter, and how incredibly adept the ECMO team was under pressure.

She looked at me with alarm. It was as if her eyes were screaming, "Do you not see your lifeless, immobilized child lying there beneath wires and IVs?"

But I truly no longer did. I saw a baby still alive. I saw soft brown hair which curled above her ears. I saw a tiny chest moving rhythmically up and down. I saw life. This woman was still at the initial stage of scratching at the jaws of death hovering above her daughter.

We did not converse for long. She could not digest my acceptance of the situation. I felt a deep compassion, but also sorrow for her, not only because she was so close to losing a child, but because she continued to fight an experience which had moved me into a soft realm of peace. I had already gone where she refused, letting my child go, and yet my child remained. How could there be a further level of fear?

Over the course of the next day, in the open expanse of the ICU, I could not help my eyes from wandering over to where this new child lay attached to the machine Sierra had relied on less than 48 hours before. The father was there often. The mother ... it was like seeing a parallel reality. It was what would have happened to me if I had successfully fled the ICU.

I was returning to the ICU with a steamed milk, because, unknown to me days before, someone said I still had to eat and live. I turned the corner to see a reverend speaking with the baby's parents. The child, a little girl, looked to be about 6 months old. I could only imagine the level of attachment. The head of the ECMO team sat at the machine looking completely spent and I sent him a wave of strength from the warm milk nestled in my hand.

I pictured the next steps this medical team would take. Silently, they would disassemble the technology, making a birth of space for the parents to hover with their child. Someone would create the foot mould. A sour taste crept into the back of my throat. The mother's tears rolled down and down as her shoulders wracked in violent sobbing. I still had to walk past to my ventilated child.

During the first days, I spat silent insults at the nurses who continued a happy banter, talking about their weekends and upcoming trips as they connected new IV bags and inserted needles. I remember angrily thinking, "How can you be so normal while my world is ending? Don't you see this?" I was still at that place of self and need, like that poor young mother who stood crying by her child. But now I could see that it was essential for the nurses and doctors to be in that state. The level of unrelenting trauma that continued to flow through the unit was not survivable without a deep sense of norm. An alter reality of sunshine and laughter needed to be ever present to balance the pain swirling in currents.

I was now in a space where this was my norm. I still ate. I still needed to walk away, out the doors of the hospital to go to my silent basement suite to sleep in order to prepare for the next day. I still felt the need to turn my face towards the sun and smile at its heat. I could laugh at a kind joke at my child's bedside and she did not die. There was to be no guilt. There was only life and a situation over which I had no control, and I needed to allow myself to be fully immersed and bathed in all that was.

By day 10, Sierra was stable enough to be moved to the Special Care Nursery into an isolated room. She was still ventilated, sedated and paralyzed, but her oxygen needs were hovering closer to 45%. Nurses and technicians prepared her apparatus for the move, and Sierra's world was wheeled down the hall with skilled precision. Any slightest jostle sent her blood pressure sailing and machines would beep warnings of dangerous increases in heart rate. A team of six wheeled her gently down the corridor, ready for any mishap. She was still touch and go, but she was holding her own beyond anything anyone had suspected.

Once positioned into the room she had been in that first fateful night, new charts were set up and new nurses were set to monitor her. A chair was in waiting for me or Mark, but mostly it held my frame. Mark could not understand my need to hover beside this child who lay unconscious and unaware, but he had not observed her change in heart rate when I whispered in her ear that I had returned from a break, or the tiny drop in blood pressure when I stroked her skin. She knew I was there and I had no other place to be … or did I?

Daniel was three years old. He was in Vancouver, blocks away while all this had transpired, but to me, a healthy, well cared for child with my mother and husband no longer registered on my radar. I had a newborn who was clinging to life, and I, in many ways, was also clinging. I had nothing to give to my son who I knew was okay. Mark would want me to leave to take Daniel to the park and I would argue that I could not go. Mark would see Sierra for 10 minutes then leave. I would see Daniel for the same. We had divided in order to meet the needs of our family and neither of us could see the rationale of the other. Bitter resentment mounted in waves.

By day 14, Dr. Singh felt Sierra was ready for the diaphragmatic hernia operation. She again had plateaued on the ventilator and the repair had to be attempted before any further respiratory gains could be made. It was unclear whether enough of the diaphragmatic muscle had developed to stretch over the hole and attach to the cartilage of the rib cage, or whether a gortex patch would need to be inserted.

As in any other industry, there are weekends. The hospital has an increased hum and activity abounds during the week, and then it grows much quieter on the weekends as only the necessities and emergencies are tended to. It was also approaching Valentine's Day and Dr. Singh argued that the operation needed be performed immediately. Other doctors argued that it could wait until the following week. All I could see was a child facing another three days without a functioning diaphragm and I could care less what day of the week it was. Mark and I wanted to scream, "Sunday, Saturday, Wednesday! Who the hell cares? If she needs this operation, do it!"

Dr. Singh is a formidable force, and we are thankful for his persistence. He pushed the issue up to the highest political level, and in the end, Sierra's operation was scheduled for Saturday, Feb. 15th at 9:00am. The head of surgery at Children's came to greet us in the waiting room and told us he would be performing the operation himself. Once again, Mark and I sat and waited for a painful 3 hours as unknown forces kept our daughter's life tethered.

There was no guarantee whether she would survive this. The liver being moved was of gravest concern and the hours following the surgery would tell a final truth. The abdominal organs would be placed back into her abdomen after developing snuggly inside her rib cage. The stomach had developed abnormally. The blood supply to her liver could be easily compromised, but the right lung needed more room to expand and this operation was the only solution.

Mark tried to keep the mood light. He was attentive. We drank coffee and steamed milk and water until I thought I would burst. We read. We conversed about Daniel and funny antics he had done the past few days. We avoided the, "what ifs" of the next few hours and to anyone else, we could have been a happy couple on a date in a different location. Yet 200 feet away our daughter was facing unimaginable physical alterations that would prove decisive.

The surgeon finally appeared down the dim lit expanse of hall. He emerged, tall and confident. Sierra had done well. Her stats remained stable and she was at 40% oxygen. We were all amazed.

Chapter 4

I will write peace on your wings
and you will fly
all over the world.

~ Sadako Sasaki

Sierra was constantly monitored on the ventilator, receiving a concoction of medications to keep her alive. All organs were vigilantly tested for degree of function and Sierra continued to battle with the aid of multiple machines.

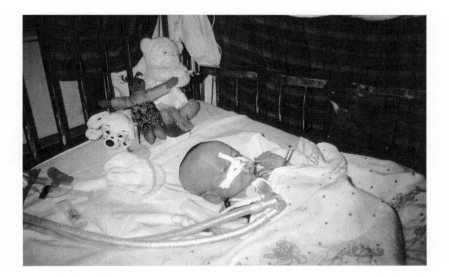

In the weeks that followed, Mark had to return home to continue running his business. He took Daniel back to the Okanagan and as two, they continued on some semblance of family life.

Daniel continued to attend his daycare. An amazing woman with a gentle, loving heart did face painting, playdough, reading and puzzles daily with my little boy. He built cushion walled forts with his friends and giggled wildly as they raced around the nest of the living room. He played in the snow, bundled safely by this woman's caring hands. For nine hours each day he ran and jumped and created, forgetting I was missing from his life. In the evening, there was his daddy to feed and bathe him, continuing our quirky family existence.

I had done my best to set up this world for him ... a world which relied completely on others. In order to provide a healthy existence for Daniel I had to give him up to the care of other people, knowing full well I was beyond depleted and unable to physically remain with him. It was as I imagine an amputation may be; still feeling the sensation of his warm, wiggly body in my arms, but removed and far away, no longer attached to me.

As a result, today Daniel is a fireball of energy … a comet blazing through my time and space, circling closer and closer if I attempt to ignore him; willing to crash in to me in order to enable my recognition of his existence.

He is a raven, curious and cunning. He is a master trickster, playfully vying for attention until he grows bored and moves on. One day this raven will morph into an owl, his wise, ageless soul settling in to watch and soar only when needed. For now, this child bird swoops in circles round my head, dropping solid, translucent pebbles to get my attention. They crackle and pop like rain around me and instead of raising my face to the spatter of drops, I shield it with my arms, afraid to get wet, not realizing the healing power of his insistent baptismal shower.

Watching him now, I wish I had had the courage to embrace my amazing little boy in each moment he appeared. I did not yet trust leaving a baby sustained by hydraulic and electrical devices, mistakenly believing I had some shred of control. If I had allowed myself to trust each moment as I was learning to do in the hospital, I would have realized that immense power was encased in the smile of my little son. His energy and power of distraction would have been rejuvenation if I had just allowed myself the permission to get swept away in his world. Instead, I gripped strongly to my narrow scope of focus, worried it may disappear if I glanced away.

During the remaining winter months, Mark and Daniel would make bi-weekly visits to see Sierra. Living in the interior, Mark had to drive four to five hours over a wintery mountain pass to return to Vancouver. Our nightly phone conversations were reduced to updates with half receptive sighs as we each relayed experiences that held no context for the other. I felt alone as sentry at Sierra's side, while Mark remained father and business owner in our previous world. As the weeks progressed, this chasm between our perspectives widened as each vantage point expanded away.

Mark's visits became a point of contention as demands I could not meet were silently communicated. I could not justify hours apart from my newborn child. Any attempts leaving Sierra to be with Mark and Daniel seemed forced, as I nervously watched the creeping clock, wondering what mishaps had occurred in my absence. Mark could not justify my resigning as a parent in Daniel's life. He challenged my reasoning for orbiting so close to the hospital's core. My conscience could see no other existence.

At a time when we needed to support each other strongly, we repelled and pushed like opposing poles. My stress would release as he drove away for another two weeks to our home.

I am not proud of these moments, but they were the staggering attempts of two wounded and floundering souls. Our mistaken singularity viscously ate away at the very sustenance we craved. Instead of reaching out and listening as one, we pitted months of pent up frustration against each other in torrents of accusations and guilt. I have heard that one of the most likely causes of divorce is the loss of a child. I truly understand the potential of this actuality. We lived it and too many times, we skated on the edge of that sliver of ice.

The rhythm of life in the hospital became my pulse. I would arrive for the 7am debriefing as the nurses changed shifts and anxiously listen as the doctor's did their rounds at 8. I would leave only for occasional pumping or coffee breaks or when a procedure was being done, and I would stay into the evening until the nurses had changed again and I was satisfied that they knew Sierra's routine.

A strange bond formed with key members of the medical team. It was like going to war, sitting in the trenches side by side in the muck and mud, the blood and the tears. We would collectively shudder as each whining bullet of unexpected crisis whizzed past our heads. Eventually, the rapid pace of fire would lull and much of the cavalry would move on, but Sierra remained an enigma and physiologically, the rules would change by the hour. The medical staff cradled my world and at times carried me forward. We had a common focus, Sierra's fight for life, and we performed a choreographed dance of pure intent and silent communion; power beyond words.

Days after Sierra's surgery, x-rays revealed the unexpected. Doctor's realized that Sierra's left lung, which had appeared so minute on initial viewing, had now expanded and could let in some air. It had been so tightly squished, it could not function when all of the other organs filled its space, but now that the chest cavity was vacant, doctors discovered that there was more left lung tissue than originally thought. The tissue of the left lobe had expanded somewhat and was assisting the right lung and that was why Sierra was doing so well. She was more stable and her oxygen needs had decreased down to an amazing 30% on the ventilator.

Due to Sierra's significant progress, Dr. Singh was considering taking Sierra off of the drug which paralyzed her and my excitement grew as I anticipated finally seeing my daughter move and open her eyes. Dr. Singh explained that the medication would be gradually reduced, but he seemed excited to be giving me the news that I would soon see my child move and catch a brief glimpse into the window of her soul.

Three weeks after her birth, Sierra finally began to move. The medication to paralyze and sedate her was gradually reduced and around 1 pm, Sierra opened her eyes. It was such a beautiful moment.

I had been waiting so long to see her eyes, it was painful. For three weeks I had stared at her physical body, but only machines gave her any animation. It is difficult to explain, but there is a communication of spirit just through silent, basic movement and it had been absent from Sierra since her birth. I felt for my husband who would not be present to see Sierra's first glimpse at the world. Unfortunately, Mark was not there to share that moment. He was due back in Vancouver on the weekend and would witness the miraculous progress she was making at that time.

The following day, I was finally able to hold Sierra. I sat carefully perched in a chair in a pale yellow sterile gown as two nurses moved Sierra and her apparatus. It was awkward as the two nurses passed her gently to me with her ventilator tube and IVs in place, but I contoured around each piece and nuzzled my daughter in my arms. It was only for a few short minutes, but it felt like heaven.

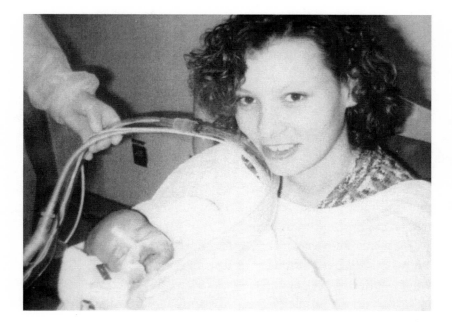

They soon moved Sierra into the Special Care Nursery with the other babies and she now had a crib instead of a sterile incubator tray on which to lie. Her oxygen levels hovered at 28% for most of the day.

The frequent suctioning of Sierra's lungs still continued as secretions continued to pool in the tissue. As they gradually reduced the morphine, Sierra developed the shakes as her body detoxed slowly from the medication. There were days when her condition was too touchy to reposition her for cuddling. Nurses were directed to reduce the midazolan and prostacyclin, which helped dilate Sierra's vascular system, but it was a delicate dance as her body adjusted to each minute change.

I would watch as the suctioning procedure occurred, as one nurse sat ready with an air bag, the other with saline drops and the suctioning tube. One would quickly detach the ventilator as the other squeezed saline down Sierra's trachea. Then the long suction tube would be quickly inserted and Sierra's little arms and legs would flail, her eyes going wide as secretions were removed from the lungs, oxygen momentarily deprived. She would cry noiselessly, as her vocal cords were impeded due to being intubated. Her heart rate and blood pressure would spike and her blood oxygen levels would dip. The other nurse would bag her with the air pump before the final suctioning took place.

I developed a routine of soothing Sierra with my voice and touch during the process as she lay fighting each step, and finally, as the long suction tube was removed and the ventilator hose back in place, I would whisper, "It's all done. It's all done," over and over as I stroked her little head in the crib, until her stats came down to her normal levels. Eventually, at a month old, Sierra learned to recognize this phrase or the tone and her little body would immediately relax, trusting that the onslaught was over.

At Sierra's four week mark, I developed a serious cold. I was not able to go visit her in the ICU as it would put her and all of the premature and ill babies at further risk. Many of the children had not developed their immune systems fully and sanitation and sterilization was necessary before ever entering the unit. Bringing in the germs of a flu or cold was warned against over and over.

It was on this day that doctors attempted to take Sierra off the ventilator. She was extubated and for one hour, they monitored her closely as she attempted to breathe on her own. She fought and fought for each shallow breath, but eventually, she succumbed from the effort. Again, they took a picture for me to see this moment, but she became so exhausted she needed to be re-intubated and life on the ventilator resumed for yet another month.

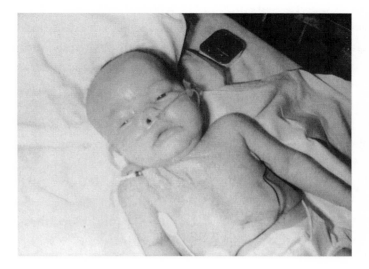

For nutrition, Sierra was being fed by a tube that snaked through her nasal passages, down her esophagus into her stomach. Her stomach was abnormal, more of a bag than a self closing container for food. With any movement or coughing, the bolus of food, which was now my pumped milk, came right back up, as she refluxed, putting her at high risk for aspirating. If any of the milk entered the trachea and reached her lungs, infection could start, setting up a possible terminal case of pneumonia. It was imperative that her lungs were not put in further jeopardy. Now, a nasal-jejunum tube was inserted, routing through the stomach into the top of the small intestine. Her feeding rate had to be reduced to allow the small intestine time to absorb and push the food along. Sierra's feeding process was a continuous daylong event. She had grown incredibly skinny, which I had not noticed until seeing the Polaroid of her off the ventilator. She needed to be gaining weight.

The next month became habitual repetition of consultations with medical staff, pumping to increase my production of breast milk, and helplessly observing as my child endured each distressing procedure. At times, the nurses would insist parents leave because it was too difficult to watch the child in anguish while the necessary intervention was carried out.

One day, Sierra had a new nurse, who was quite young and new to the world of neonatal care. During rounds, which I had missed that morning, the issue of Sierra's stomach secretions being regurgitated and causing aspiration issues was discussed and it was recommended that an additional tube be inserted through Sierra's other nostril to drain the stomach of bile.

As I arrived, the nurse was just starting the procedure. She started explaining to me what she was doing and inserted a brightly coloured tube into Sierra's nose. Immediately, Sierra went into panic, as her nasal passageways were being invaded yet again. The nurse continued to insert the tube into Sierra's stomach and Seirra's heart rate began to climb. She flailed her six week old arms and panic flashed through her little eyes again and again.

The nurse became increasingly concerned as we watched Sierra's heart rate continue to climb, approaching 200 beats per minute. She called over the respiratory therapist to monitor her blood oxygen levels which were decreasing with each minute. Sierra continued to fight, flailing and silently crying past the ventilator tube. I restrained myself as best I could, for I had learned that as a parent, if you display too much emotion, you would be removed from your child during the medical procedure and asked to return once calm prevailed.

I steadily asked the nurse if this additional tube was absolutely necessary, considering the distress it was causing. She said she has been directed to insert it and it may not be the reason for Sierra's distress. I used every ounce of my self restraint not to rip the tube out myself as I saw Sierra's heart rate crest 200 beats per minute. Finally, the distraught nurse called over a doctor who was with another child. I could wait no longer.

I cut in abruptly saying I had been with Sierra constantly and that this drop in oxygen and increase in heart rate was not normal and was initiated when the second tube had been inserted. The doctor turned to the nurse and said, "Then pull it out."

Like that, she followed instructions and removed the tube. Immediately Sierra's crying calmed and her heart rate began a steady decent to more normal levels. I stood shaking softly as I watched the numbers creep down on the monitor and her oxygen levels resumed their norm. I raced out of the SCN and went to the washroom where I began to cry, physically ill from the distress and overwhelmed by the frustration and panic of the situation.

I began to realize that my non-medical parental knowledge of my child was just as crucial in her survival as all of the medication and medical guess work involved and I needed to keep my composure and presence in order to ensure Sierra's survival. I shuddered to think that if I had arrived a half hour later, Sierra's heart rate and distress could have triggered a cardiac arrest. It reinforced my resolve to remain with her for each moment of this ordeal.

Parenthood…
It is an infinite love in a finite reality,
that is the painful part.

-unknown

Chapter 5

Sierra's graduation to the Special Care Nursery from the ICU brought a decline in adrenaline as I realized she had successfully weathered a month and was improving each day. My panic-restricted view was gradually widening and I had hours to observe the amazing little lives surrounding me.

We were in an open area with ten to twelve babies and my chair fit right beside another incubator. It was impossible not to watch these other children just feet away. For a while, the baby immediately to the right of Sierra was being monitored by the same nurse and it was a volley of procedures between the two. The baby was only 27 weeks old and tinier than any human I had ever seen. His skin was translucent and one could trace each tiny blood vessel beneath the surface. He was muscle, skin and bone as he had not had time to gain his protective layers of fat in the womb. Incredibly, I could also see the ridges of the baby's cerebral cortex as the bones of the skull had not yet fully formed. This amazing baby had spunk and spirit as he moved ten tiny fingers and toes, softly crying and letting his presence be known. I would stare in silent wonder at this miniature being, and respectfully avert my eyes when the parents were allowed to reach in and touch their little one.

As parents, we all had the common bond of the SCN. The normal rules of engagement in society outside of the hospital walls did not apply. Virtual strangers would ask intimate questions and they could relate to this experience unfolding simultaneously for us all. The most pronounced moment happened one day while I was in the parents' waiting area while Sierra endured yet another procedure.

I was sitting, reading my half hearted choice of well-read magazines when a mother started a conversation like so many others.

"How is your baby doing?" she said quietly as she settled herself in the chair.

"Fairly well. How about yours?" I replied, happy for the human contact.

"Our little guy is doing okay. He's 33 weeks and he's having an operation tomorrow."

I looked at her fully now. "Is it going to be a long one?"

"Four hours. They are operating on his heart." Her eyes glanced down.

A stillness swept over me. "He will be okay. They are all amazing here." I said of the doctors and nursing staff.

She nodded and folded her own magazine in her hand. "Your baby's been very strong through her operations, too." She stated.

I looked at her with puzzled curiousity. "Yes, she has. How do you know?"

"I was there that first night." She said, our eyes communicating the silent terror and sadness of that scene.

I looked at her for a long time, and then she reached over and hugged me, beginning to cry. She whispered. "You are both so strong. It must have been so frightening."

I hugged her back just as hard, this stranger who had shared my worst moment. When we released, we were as old friends, silently sending strength and quiet understanding to the other. Fate was colliding our lives together in ferocious ways and our bond was the shared title of mother.

A tall nurse came to the door to tell me that I could return to Sierra as the procedure was done. The woman next to me nodded and said, "You need to go."

I nodded back. "Your little guy will do well tomorrow."

She nodded again and I moved away.

I never did learn her name, but I will always recognize her soul.

My comfort and familiarity with the ward grew quietly. Once a confusing maze of hallways, doors and buzzers, I maneuvered assuredly through the areas to my little girl. Nurses knew me as "Baby Robinson's mom" and they would call through from the nursing station as I approached to let me in. My hands were growing raw and tight from the scrubbing, little cracks forming on my skin as I lathered with other parents at the long metal sink, our collective suds merging as the water swept down the drain. I would gather the newly printed labels from the nurses for my milk and check in for my day.

The pumping room was more hospitable in the SCN, set up with four comfortable chairs for mothers. If we hadn't all been numb and in a state of shock, it could have appeared odd or comical to us, as we hooked up to machines, baring our breasts to total strangers. The two pairs of chairs faced each other and we all became adept at opening the plastic sterile packages and hooking up to the apparatus. The rhythmic whir and clunk of the weighted pendulum of the machine would be a backdrop for the next twenty minutes as we sat and watched the drops pool into the plastic vials. I felt for new mothers who had never experienced the joy of breastfeeding a warm suckling baby. To associate these machines as the only experience of breastfeeding would undoubtedly end many attempts to stick it out. At least I could remember when I would nuzzle Daniel and how his little fists would knead at the sides to get more milk to flow down. I smiled at the image often as the mechanism now whirred away.

As I placed the morning's collections into the fridge, I saw Dr. Solimano and he said he was hoping to show something new to me. This man I now trusted explicitly moved me towards a side room for more X-ray viewing.

Today, he stared at the stomach, a funny shaped bag now below the chest. He explained that the muscles which usually tightened at the base of the esophagus, to ensure the food remained in the stomach, were not functioning in Sierra. Eventually, they would need to do an operation, called a fundal placation to tighten this opening to help reduce the amount of reflux. He described how if this did not suffice, Sierra may need to be tube fed directly through a tube into her stomach, but he said that would be "down the road."

I liked the phrase "down the road" because my nerves had had enough of "minute by minute" and it hinted at a sense of permanence. The question of whether Sierra would survive was not glaring at me daily any longer, rather, we were figuring out the terms and conditions of her survival, which I was more than happy to embrace.

Many months before when I was still pregnant, a close friend of ours had offered us his basement suite in Vancouver when he heard of the challenges we would be facing with the baby. By some mysterious providence, we discovered that his home was only four blocks away from Children's Hospital in a beautiful, secluded area. The street almost led directly to the front door of Children's Hospital.

Morning walks to the hospital were silent. I walked through an older area of the city with full grown oaks and an open expanse of grass across a quiet park. Light dew would caress my shoes as I moved across the damp sod. The sun would be rising and a gradual light would touch each tree on my approach. Peace pervaded this part of my day and I would replenish as I approached closer to Sierra's world. I would review tiny moments of the day before and cherish a look or a smile from complete strangers. Yet, without fail, all too suddenly the hectic pulse of the traffic would eventually assault my ears and my peaceful introspective journey would come to an abrupt end.

One particular morning, after I had entered the hospital's hum, I carried a coffee and set it down carefully to attend to the ritual of hand scrubbing. Familiar nurses and other parents glanced brief hello's as we again began our bizarre routines in lives no one could have predicted. I patted dry with the beige paper towels and picked up the coffee, still scalding hot.

I entered through the heavy metal doors once the nurse buzzed me in and went through the next portal to the busy SCN. What I was about to discover stopped me cold.

Her crib was gone.

My heart seized inside my chest as the scalding coffee wobbled and scorched my hand. My mind froze, but a deeper part of me grasped for logic. If something had happened to her in the night, they would have phoned. I stayed only blocks away. They would have called. My sight remained riveted to the open expanse of floor. The void of space violently sucked at my soul. I forced my legs to move towards the area where she had once been and my voice cracked as I turned to a nurse.

"Sierra…the baby who was here," my eyes welled with pain. "What happened?"

"Oh, Sierra." The nurse stated as she continued adjusting the lines to a premature boy. "During rounds this morning, they assessed her and…"

My throat closed completely. I could no longer breathe.

"They decided to move her to another area because she is progressing so well."

I inhaled audibly and my coffee began to quiver wildly in my hand. "Another room?"

I squeaked, still trying to register her words. "She's okay?"

"She's doing great." The nurse smiled, so unaware of my moments of horror.

I exhaled and turned to search out my child. A part of me would not resume function until I visually registered her form. I followed murky directions, desperately searching out her new locale and entered a dimly lit room with less activity. Immediately I recognized the blanket shading one side of her crib. Rounding the side, my eyes drank in her tiny, baby form, little eyes blinking innocently at the lights. I threw out the coffee and reached to feel some solidity, gently squeezing her tiny arm. Slowly it began to process. She was there. She was real. She was safe.

The new nurse said a cheerful good morning, briefing me on Sierra's night. She must have thought me mute because I had yet to remember how to speak, my body's faculties slowly returning. The panic elicited during the previous minutes had vaulted me into a realm I wished to never revisit and I slowly returned to my usual state.

Sierra blinked unknowingly and gazed silently at the colourful bits of her surroundings. I continued to touch her arm, not able to break contact. Shock slowly dissipated from my system as I watched her little movements. I wound a little musical toy and let it play beside her, the twang of each note settling my fear.

The nurse rattled off some changes in medication, but I was in a trance with the child's tune playing round my daughter's head, watching her eyes dance back and forth. Eventually, I came to and was able to carry on some semblance of normal conversation with the friendly woman tending my child, but the sudden shock and false sense of loss still reverberated through my body for another hour.

I know the pace of the ward is intense, but someone should have thought to communicate the change of location to the relative visiting. I let it slip by, but that sickening moment still flares from time to time.

As part of a support for parents, doctors and nurses often attempted to partner families who were experiencing similar circumstances, with their children battling the same diseases or conditions. Our nurse had told us of a young couple whose little boy also had congenital diaphragmatic hernia and was about 3 months older than Sierra. It was such a rare condition we jumped at the chance to speak with them.

Mark and I met Melody and Sean during an evening visit with our little girl, while she slept peacefully. They were inspiring beyond words as they shared the story of their first born son and his complicated journey. Again, all of society's false pretences were negated as we merged on levels of truth and bare trust.

My curiosity grew to learn more about their son, Ryan. He became a beacon of hope, knowing that he had survived this ordeal and was growing and meeting new mile stones. Speaking with Melody during mornings in the ward provided a strong sense of hope and camaraderie as we shared events the children had faced the day before. Melody had waited twice as long as I had before she could hold her son. There were differences in the path each child had taken, but the similarities and challenges they faced were like mirrored images down a long tunnel, with Ryan leading the way.

On a particularly challenging day, when a child psychologist had come through to test Sierra's intellectual abilities and Sierra had failed the simple tracking tests miserably, I left the hospital to walk to the closest grocery store and get some air.

It always struck me as ridiculously odd that at one moment, I could be immersed in this frightening reality with my daughter so ill and the next I could enter the sunshine and be engulfed by the swirling world of the city, completely ignorant of my plight.

During the first weeks, I would stand dumbfounded in the lineup at the grocery store as I impatiently counted off each second between buying my food and returning to Sierra's side. On one trip, I remember observing the absurdity of a woman arguing with the cashier over the validity of a coupon for 50 cents off an item. Less than 300 yards away, my daughter's every breath was being mechanically set into motion. When it was my turn, the cashier uttered the standard, "So, how is your day going?"

I could only mutter a standard, "Fine."

It seemed unbelievable to me that the world continued to function, regardless of individual crisis or cracked realities. At the time, I did not understand the significance, but I slowly came to realize that I was the only one judging whether my current experiences were nightmarish or not. If I chose to remain paralyzed in fear and self-pity, I would begin a decent into a depression from which I may never emerge. If I remained optimistic and searched hard for the special treasures in each day, I would view this experience in a completely different light. It was my choice as to which filter I viewed my world.

On this grocery trip, I decided to do something for Melody, to bring some cheer to her day. Mine was off to a terrible start, but I needed a new focus to divert my concentration off my worries. I went into the grocery and floated between the buds and flowers in the floral department. Spring was still approaching, but these forced blooms held colours rich in hope and inspiration. Bright yellows and delicate pinks took graceful shape before my eyes, and I forced myself to smell each bouquet. Eventually, I picked the yellow daffodils and asked to have them wrapped with baby's breath … the irony only hitting me now.

I walked back to the hospital in a new frame of mind. Nothing had changed, circumstances remained the same, but my outlook had switched from wallowing in my thickening despair to feeling the breeze and anticipating Melody's smile when she saw the daffodils. I felt lighter than I had in days.

As expected, Melody looked at me with buoyant surprise and my spirits rose with her instant smile. Incredulously, she took the six flowers from me and began to explain that Ryan was having a rough day. His nitric oxide levels had to be increased, which in many ways felt like a step backwards. I could see the dark circles being etched on her young face and I was so glad I had taken the time to find her the flowers. Such an innocent, tiny act had given us both the strength to face the rest of the muddled day with our children.

Over the next few weeks, tiny steps of progress were made. The medical team had warned us that one of the common side effects of being on ECMO was loss of hearing. It occurred in over 60% of the children who needed the technology. While Sierra was only two months old, a hearing specialist came in to do testing of her auditory reception. Unbelievably, they could do some of the testing while Sierra was asleep. They placed tiny nodules in her ears and hooked up sensors on her head. I don't fully understand how it worked, but they could monitor neurological reactions to the sounds being played. Even if Sierra's hearing checked out as normal at the moment, the loss of hearing after ECMO was often a gradual event, with the hearing loss becoming progressively worse throughout the toddler years. The reasoning for this was still just speculation, but doctors believed it was somehow related to the lack of oxygen and damage to the auditory nerves in the brain.

Sierra was slowly gaining weight by increasing her tube feeds and she could have a bath in a silver bowl once all of the cardiac sensors had been temporarily removed and her oxygen tubing was stretched over to accommodate the activity.

Sierra loved the water. She would relax in the warmth as we sudsed her sinuous little shape. The nurses had invented a type of spa for Sierra, by taking an extra hose and attaching it to a spare oxygen outlet, which created bubbles when placed in the water. Sierra loved it and I laughed at the decadence of it all. I could think of no one more deserving.

Each morning at rounds, the doctors had now begun to include me, realizing my role as historian. Doctors were scheduled on three week cycles, and when a new neonatologist entered Sierra's world, I became the constant. She had some regular nurses, but these had varied between each move between units and, for a reason I had not thought about.

At one point, I had asked a nurse in the Special Care Nursery if she could be Sierra's primary nurse, but her wisdom blindsided me. She declined and explained that being a primary nurse had proven too painful too many times, for the nurses get too attached to the little ones, then, if something tragic should occur, it is as if they too have lost a child. I had not considered this. So in the end, Sierra had a rotation of nurses and again, I was the historian, up to date on the most recent dosage changes and alterations in medication.

Sierra had amassed an incredible three and a half files of records in her two months, and it was impossible for each new player to memorize each bit of information they contained. I had been able to summarize critical issues. After listening to close to 40 sessions of daily rounds, I knew what information the medical team was looking for and could add my observations as to what percentages and behaviour was normal for Sierra.

Mark visited frequently, once bringing in his parents who traveled out from Ontario. My mom and 89 year old grandmother came in to provide support as well. Few visitors were allowed into the sacred, sterile area with so many tiny souls fighting for their existence, but having familiar faces enter this isolated world was like nourishment for my draining, parched spirit.

One quiet afternoon, while my grandmother held Sierra, I could feel her healing energy swirl around my daughter. My grandmother had beautiful, mystical eyes with a dark blue ring circling her brown iris. Her silky chocolate skin was etched with intricately unique designs that only a long, well traversed life can arrange. Jamaican's cherish children and a beautiful peace settled over my grandmother as she held my ailing child.

My grandmother believed each spirit continued to thrive in a realm beyond ours' after death. She permeated a relaxed, accepting calm of this belief, yet I know she treasured being able to share this tangible moment with Sierra.

The doctors at Children's Hospital do an incredible job of monitoring the health and well being of the entire family. They know how essential it is and how, in a crisis, every family member becomes a patient to some degree. Doctors were very aware that I was also a mother to a three year old boy living in the interior and they were cognizant of my desire to be reunited. I had inquired several times whether a transfer to Kelowna General Hospital would be a possibility considering the progress Sierra was making. Very kindly, doctors would explain that it was essential they not jump the gun and transfer Sierra before she was ready, as she was still in very fragile condition and her status remained random at best.

Looking back now, Children's Hospital and the caring environment there was exactly what both Sierra and I needed. As it would turn out, you do need to be very careful what you wish for.

When we are motivated by goals
that have deep meaning,
by dreams that need completion,
by pure love that needs expressing,
then we truly live life.

~ Greg Anderson

Chapter 6

As a child, I was very determined and persistent. My creativity to ensure I got my own way drove my mother mad. She tells stories where I would be sent to my room for punishment and I would either make the best of my new situation and find fabulous ways to entertain myself or the time when at four, I decided to leave through the window and go to a neighbour's home and proceeded to make cookies. My refusal to accept a punishment or consequence as negative infuriated my mother to no end.

It was only during my time immersed in the struggle with Sierra that I realized how much of a gift my personality was, almost as if I was meant to practice those mental survival skills from day one in preparation for this child's journey.

No matter what was thrown at me growing up, I would search for a creative outlet in that space, always satiating the curious nature of my mind. This isn't to say I never grew frustrated, but something deeper would initiate and a situation that for most would be enough to squelch their spirit, would become a challenge to find the hidden route to discovery for me.

It was precisely this aspect of my nature that allowed me to mentally survive Sierra's ordeal.

By her eight week mark, doctors were well aware that I was pushing for a move to the hospital in our home town as soon as Sierra was stable enough. My guilt mounted each week I was away from Daniel and in my narrow scope of rationale, I believed the move closer to home would be the answer to mending the hole in my life created by this separation from my son.

By week eleven, Sierra had been off oxygen for ten days. I did not have the courage to share this fact with Melody, for Ryan was still on oxygen and nitric oxide supplementation, but when she stopped in for a visit at Sierra's crib one morning, she saw the progress for herself. I saw the flash of confusion and could only imagine the natural feeling of injustice at the pace of Sierra's advancement in comparison to her own son. I felt a need to shield her from the truth, but it was there in front of her now. Melody was congratulatory, but the visit was short. I could imagine the feelings of injustice pulling deeply at Melody for the rest of the day as she sat with her child.

The doctors gave the go ahead for Sierra's move to Kelowna and the process of transfer and debriefing the Pediatrician who would be responsible for her care in the Okanagan began. Once again, my false belief that my mind could fathom every element and variable of this new situation gave me an artificial sense of control.

The infant transfer team was notified of Sierra's pending move in the next week and one of the surgeons from the ECMO operation was requested to remove an existing shunt still embedded in Sierra's neck. In the grand scheme of the events in the SCN, this was a minor detail that I'm sure barely registered with the surgeons' hectic schedules.

The week was a blur as I packed up my simple life at the basement suite into my one bag and prepared for my return home. Sierra was by no means, "out of the woods", but the doctors felt that in light of the needs of the whole family, her condition was strong enough to endure the move to the facility in Kelowna, although operations and assessments would need to be conducted back at Children's Hospital in Vancouver.

Sierra was still in frequent need of suctioning, her blood oxygen levels were constantly being monitored, she was on a feeding tube with food continuing to bypass her stomach and being deposited into the small intestine. She would eventually need an operation to be put on a feeding tube that could be inserted externally through her abdomen into her jejunum. She would also need the fundal placation operation that Ryan was going through at that very moment, to tighten the top of the stomach to stop the constant reflux of food back up the esophagus, posing the deadly threat of aspiration to the lungs. Intellectually, the hope for Sierra was hovering close to mild intellectual delay as initial assessments were conducted and reviewed. Yet, I still pushed for the move, completely unaware of the capacity of the destined unit.

Mark recently had visited, seeing Sierra off oxygen for himself. When I relayed the news that we may soon be transferred closer to home, he was just as relieved.

We both believed the move would finally bring us closer to a normal family existence. It is humbling to look back and see how different individual perceptions and expectations can be when trying to quell an individual need.

The transfer to Kelowna was set for a Thursday, and the Infant Transfer Team of paramedics and the computerized incubator complete with oxymeter and cardiac monitoring equipment was primed for containing this still fragile baby. We all sat in a holding pattern as we patiently awaited the surgeon to remove the shunt before the move. Frustration had grown over the week as transfer was delayed once due to the pending removal of the shunt and discovering that the minor procedure had been cancelled and rescheduled. On this current afternoon, in the dim light of the ward, we once again received the news that the procedure was cancelled, but the doctors' decided that Sierra would be moving to Kelowna with the shunt still in place. The incision site on her neck would need to be monitored closely as signs of infection were detected.

The transfer team placed Sierra, now in one of the two sleepers I had allowed myself to purchase before her birth, into the incubator and the familiar wires were placed sequentially to provide the constant monitoring while in the air.

Nurses wished us well as the transport incubator was wheeled down the hall with my scores of milk vials and they proceeded out to the ambulance which would take the team to the airport. I followed proudly with my one bag, so eager to see my home again after three months.

When we reached the tar-mac, the plane wasn't ready for flight. Sheets of rain spattered fiercely off the runway and the transport teams' frustration grew as they waited for the pilot to give the go ahead to board.

During the wait, I was introduced to a woman and her child, also coming from Children's who were catching a ride to Kamloops on our way to the Okanagan. The young mother with blond hair remarked that her baby had a rare disorder called diaphragmatic hernia. I froze. She continued that it had been a long two weeks in hospital, but now her son was ready to go home. He sucked easily on a bottle and no oxygen was needed for the flight.

My mind churned on so many levels. Ugly jealousy rose violently to the surface as I processed what she now said. Her son had a mild case of the disorder and a bitter rage at the injustice stirred with my ego. I quickly caught this and berated myself for thinking in such a dreadfully selfish manner and allowed this woman to complete her story, communicating how scary and difficult it had been. I made myself still and dug deep for compassion that usually spilled so naturally. I did not tell her Sierra had the same condition, only that she had respiratory issues, and I silently vowed to never share this story with Melody, thinking it could crush her.

Once in the air, the transport team maintained a relaxed banter as they efficiently monitored Sierra's stats. We soon touched down in Kamloops, and I wished the woman and her baby well, allowing myself to breath cleansing air and feel a sense of empathy for their plight. The door soon closed and my eyes settled once again on my daughter, little eyes blinking so innocently and unknowing, and pain sank like a stone in the pit of my stomach.

The flight to Kelowna went by quickly and an ambulance was waiting on the tarmac to take Sierra and I on the final leg to the hospital. During the ride, I shared some information about Sierra's normal SpO2 levels, and the paramedic looked surprised. I simply said I had picked up a lot during her stay at Children's.

I'll never forget our arrival at Kelowna General. Kind nurses wheeled in IV poles to the isolated room where Sierra would stay. I was surprised to learn of the isolation status, forgetting how susceptible she was to any respiratory virus. The Pediatric ward was much quieter than the SCN, but that was only one of many differences. I watched closely as they hooked Sierra up to each new machine after being removed from the transport incubator. As we all watched her stats, we soon discovered her respiratory gains at Children's were not enough to cope with the change in altitude in Kelowna and Sierra was once again hooked up to the oxygen tubes, a part of me deflating as they adjusted the dial.

The reality of the move quickly settled and I soon felt the heavy weight of the demands around me. Unbeknownst to me, I had been gently sheltered while in Vancouver. Despite the chaos and urgency of it all, I had silent moments of reprieve which had nourished my spirit. In my eagerness to return to my family, I had not considered all of the ramifications. In every circumstance, there are human dynamics which we often fail to consider. Every human being with whom we come into contact has some expectation, and some demands cannot be met when one has been mentally and physically deplenished.

Mark and Daniel, as well as Mark's parents met Sierra and I at the hospital once she was settled. Tears and joy bound us together as glossy eyes gazed longingly at each other. I swooped Daniel into my arms, but being three, he was not there for long.

After a visit and catching up, Mark and his parents were ready to go, but were surprised when I said I was not coming home. I did not want to leave Sierra alone in this room on the first night. The rules of the game had changed. This hospital was not equipped with a personal nurse for each child and I abruptly realized that the expectation was for a parent to be present with the child at all times.

Mark immediately let his opinion be known, that it was the job of the nurses to meet the needs of the patient, and that I could not be expected to be there every night. The truth was, my family and I had all believed I would be returning home, to resume my role as mother and wife, but it was becoming increasingly clear that the situation, instead of easing, was about to take on an entirely new and extra dimension. Thus, not even three hours into my return, Mark and I drew our lines in the sand and once again set up two different camps of thought.

I conceded to go to dinner with them all, as Sierra was sleeping, but my nervousness at leaving this tiny child with someone only checking in on her mounted with each moment. Mark's dad agreed with him, taking the perspective that it was the nurses' job to be with Sierra. The policy of the pediatric ward was not so. I am not saying anyone was in the wrong, it was just a different environment with different resources and expectations and I'm unsure as to whether the medical team at Children's Hospital realized the distinction. I now knew this ward was not staffed to provide the level of care and attention we had been receiving.

I spent the first night with Sierra in her new, isolated room on the plastic fold down chair with a thin blanket, barely sleeping as nurses changed her feeding bags, checked her stats and temperature, and pressed the buttons on machines all through the night.

I began a descent into a murky realm of guilt, knowing that as a mother in regular circumstances, I would be up at all hours, exhausted with my infant anyways. But, so many dynamics were not being considered.

As a family, we had just experienced over 60 days of intense, life threatening trauma. I had endured living in a strange environment, away from much of my network of support. If the circumstances had been normal, I would be caring for my child in my own home, which provides a strong sense of relaxation and comfort. Instead, I was constantly surrounded by strangers, who all meant well, but became entrenched players in our lives every waking hour of every day.

The situation in Vancouver had provided a reprieve at the end of each day to replenish and refocus, centering myself for the next day's unexpected twists. Now, the hospital's silently communicated expectation was that I be there 24/7, as each other parent was with their children with broken legs or an appendix being removed. The fact is, each of those parents were coming in "fresh", out of their normal lives, for maybe four to seven days.

We were easily facing another one to two months of hospitalization before Sierra would be transported back to Children's to get her stomach operation. The added twist was, Mark had every expectation that I would be home again each evening, helping with our son during dinner and bedtime. I felt stretched like over pulled taffy and soon something would give and I would crack into a thousand pieces.

I did my best to create some balance, but there was no pleasing everyone involved, and unfortunately, I was still young and naïve enough to think it was my job in life to make everyone else happy and live up to their expectations.

Daniel continued to go to his daycare in the mornings. I would try to get to the hospital, now a 35 minute drive away, by 7 or 8 in the morning. I would stay with Sierra until about 3 when she would again be sleeping, than head to the next town to pick Daniel up from daycare, then head with him sleeping, back to the hospital, where our adjusted family routine would continue until Mark came in after long days at work to relieve me around 6 and I would take Daniel home to prepare dinner. Some evenings, I would stay with Sierra, but I would be so exhausted from the night's activities with nurses doing rounds and buzzers ringing on machines, that I frequently got sick and was be unable to be with Sierra without a mask and gown and intense sterilization.

Daniel was getting increasingly frustrated with my presence. I think it was almost worse on him with me being there than when I was out of sight in Vancouver. I had no energy to play with him and the time we spent together was always doing necessary chores or being cooped together in the hospital room. I would constantly be getting angry at him for touching things in the room or hanging off the side of the metal crib. He would want to touch the buttons on the feeding regulator and I would shout for him to get away. He had very limited space on the floor to drive his cars and would soon grow board and want to leave.

Times when Sierra would cry and I needed to pick her up, tubes and wires and all, Daniel would clamor for my hands and do anything he could for my attention. Amidst all of this, a nurse would walk in and say it was time for me to change Sierra's feeding bag, blatantly ignoring the dysfunctional family scene erupting around her.

Nights when I did go home, Mark and I would fight about how "unrealistic" my being at the hospital was and I would fall into bed exhausted, often crying, only to do it again for another 60+ days.

There isn't much more to share about this period. Suffice it to say, the move to Kelowna turned a very difficult circumstance into a living nightmare where I felt insufficient, depleted and distressed beyond anything I had ever experienced. Our return to Children's in mid May for Sierra's scheduled fundal placation surgery was hoped to be a welcome reprieve.

It has become appallingly obvious
that our technology
has exceeded our humanity.

~ Albert Einstein

Chapter 7

We returned to Vancouver in early May. An ambulance transported Sierra and me from Kelowna to the airport where she was loaded on to the air transport plane. Once again a medical team accompanied us on the flight to Vancouver airport where another ambulance waited to take Sierra to Children's Hospital. Sierra was two months older and I walked with my head high feeling some sense of success entering the doors onto the premise where my daughter was born. That night was buried so deep in my psyche, I wished it never to return, and I escorted a four month old child into the space where death had once hovered so near.

I can't describe the sense of coming home … for it was still a hospital, but each familiar face I met welcomed us with hope as they recognized Sierra and saw the advancement she had made.

Naively, I had thought we would be returning to the warmth and safety of the Special Care Nursery, but Sierra was older and had been exposed to another hospital, so she needed to be admitted to the pediatric ward on the third floor. This came as a surprise, as I was expecting we would be dealing with the same doctors who knew Sierra from birth, but brand new individuals entered the scene from every corner of the stage.

It seemed in some way she had become a case of interest as she had overcome what many thought to be insurmountable odds. Those who studied neonatal development wanted to see her progress for themselves. I realized that her survival represented an incredible opportunity to examine the elements of what went right during the management of her initial delicate condition in the Intensive Care Unit and that possibly much could be learned, but a part of me resented the fact that my child, a living breathing being, was just an interesting case study on a pile of files in scores of offices. People from professions I didn't even know existed were introduced to us each day and my head whirled with the dazzling pace of dialogues and exams.

In contrast, there was a lot of alone time too. I sat on a seat beside Sierra's bed in a room with three other parents and their children ... I should say two other parents. If I had learned anything through my experience in the hospitals, it was not to judge the choices of another human being. We have no way of comprehending the extent of human suffering and anguish that one goes through during these "feats of scientific genius". Only the individuals involved fully understand all of the extenuating circumstances. In the long silence, I pondered philosophical issues; truths centering on the ethics of using all of our technological advances to enable survival. We are indebted to every invention and apparatus that allowed our child to prolong her fight to live, but many days, as I sat amongst the parents and tiny children who would be facing incredible challenges and disabilities for the rest of their lives, I questioned who we were doing this for.

Science is allowing us to cross so many lines. We have been blessed to be one of the lucky families to have a child due to these advances, but days when I sat silently watching the scenes around me, I questioned the methods. Should infants have to endure such torment? Should we have the right to prolong lives even though the little ones are suffering and in so much pain they must be placed into a coma to endure? My child would not be here but for technology and we are indebted to so many.

Sierra was hooked up to machinery, electronic leads positioned strategically to read her ECG and respiratory rate. The familiar canary yellow feeding tube was taped firmly through her nostril. The neonatal development team came by in waves to see her progress and I puffed my chest out like a mother duck when the neonatal development team came to do their assessment.

Two months before, it had been this same Occupational Therapist and Psychologist who had assessed Sierra and their initial results had indicated that my child would most likely be moderately intellectually delayed. Now they shook their heads in amazement at the milestones we had ensured Sierra met. Sierra was grasping, tracking, and making monosyllabic sounds, right on pace with her peers. The child Mark and I had observed and coached all along was finally testing to the degree that no one believed was possible.

I kept thanking our intuitive drive for not giving up on stimulating her senses like a normal infant. All of the music we had played, the talking we had done, the singing, the cuddling, the moving her hands so she could feel the sensation of grasping textured objects, desensitizing her face, using high contrast visuals in her crib.... it had all worked. She was delayed but responding and it had all worked.

The surgical team stopped by to appraise whether Sierra was ready for the fundal placation surgery. After briefly assessing her and reading her chart, they ventured off to confer. There were usually at least two interns in tow and again my head spun as people were introduced with respective titles attached.

I told myself that it was a valuable learning experience. I tried to remain positive and see it as an incredible learning experience for many who were just starting in the medical field, but at times it became difficult to embrace their presence. Too often they made comments as to the "theoretical percentages of the presenting diagnosis" as the basis for their discussion, and they would talk hypothetically around my child's bedside, rather than just focusing on my child. I had to restrain my desire to ask them to focus on the little bundle of energy wiggling in front of them instead of discussing medical journal statistics.

Time is a fleeting entity to the surgeons and I appreciate their hectic schedules, but I hope that, during some moments, they do actually see the person in front of them and sense their presence. It is not all theory and we fool ourselves into believing it is so. There are dynamics much more powerful than what we can measure scientifically. I believe at times we all sense this, but our society believes in tangible proof, almost to our detriment.

Every little life has its own healing capabilities and these play just as vital a role in each procedure as the skilled and highly educated surgeons who mold the fragile body into a better functioning mass. I hope, for all physicians, each case maintains a face and a spirit to guide each decision being made.

Due to the two ventrical septal defects in Sierra's heart, she was at moderate risk for an infection called bacterial endocarditis. This was a consideration with the surgical procedure they were about to perform, as an infection could greatly jeopardize her survival. Sierra was still quite underweight, but she was growing well with the tube feeding. As she developed greater skills grasping and increased mobility, she was pulling the feeding tube loose more and more frequently. Part of the operation to tighten the top of her stomach also involved creating an opening through the exterior of her abdomen and placing in a "Mic Key" attachment that would become her feeding route. After this procedure, Sierra would have an exterior tube going straight into her stomach which we would hook tubes to every several hours to administer a feed. This would eventually enable Sierra to go home, after we were taught how to operate the machinery.

Sierra was temporarily on oxygen again due to the flight down to the coast, and the change in altitude. She was connected to an oxymeter to monitor her blood oxygen levels. The machine could not get an accurate reading if the patient moved too much, and as a four month old, Sierra was beginning to move all the time. Throughout the night, as I attempted to get comfortable on the rickety thin mattress cot, the buzzer for her alarm would go off continuously. It would wake the other sets of parents and children in the room and I would constantly be jumping up to momentarily mute the machine. Nurses would quickly come in each time to assess her. I had been through this enough to realize the sporadic low readings the oxymeter was registering were not Sierra's true oxygen levels, as she was doing well and was not cyanotic. The nurses had been strictly instructed to continuously monitor her respiratory status and could not disconnect the machine. Each time Seirra moved considerably, the oxygen level would read abnormally low.

It became an exhausting four days as the final pre-surgery assessments continued and I waited for her surgery to be announced. There was a young baby right across the room from us who was soon going to be returning home. His mother had shared some of his story with me and eventually, I shared some of Sierra's experience.

As the family packed up to leave the next morning, the surgeon came in to see me and said that he didn't feel Sierra was physically strong enough for the Fundal Placation surgery, due to several reasons, including her touchy respiratory status. It was too dangerous to put her under anesthetic which would further inhibit her respiration.

I felt crushed, as we had been flown to Vancouver specifically for the procedure which would enable us to bring our child home. The surgeon said they would need to delay it for another one or two months.

I maintained my composure as the surgeon left, but minutes later when the next set of visiting physicians came in to look at Sierra, I broke down. This team was the neonatologist and physiotherapist with interns in tow. Several of the people I had never met before, but there I was crying in front of them as I explained the news of the delayed operation. I quietly stated that I didn't know how much longer I could keep this up. The neonatologist who I had met several times took me aside. He said that even though I was the only adult there in Vancouver to care for Sierra, it was crucial that I take time for myself to go for walks and clear my head.

The familiar black cloak of guilt enveloped me. To leave the build-ing without my child seemed sinful, but it became imperative that I also take care of myself. When the follow up team left, I had stopped crying and wasn't as embarrassed as I would have thought. Our lives had become so public I was beginning to grow accustomed to showing my deepest emotions in front of absolute strangers. People seemed to be ever present.

As I sat quietly beside Sierra's raised bed, the woman and man from across the room approached with their little boy. They had been discharged and were all set to go. They showed a rainbow coloured stuffed bunny to me and explained that they had bought it in the gift store downstairs to bring Sierra luck. I began to tear up again. Their thoughtfulness was so poignant and I thanked them with a crooked smile as they placed the rabbit on the bed beside Sierra.

Again, I don't know their names, but it was such a touching, timely gesture and I appreciated their generosity.

Before we left the hospital to be flown back to Kelowna, I insisted that the shunt in Sierra's neck be removed. The infection which came on and off was dangerous to Sierra because of her heart condition due to the risk of developing bacterial endocarditis. The surgeon said that it could be done the following day.

A surgeon who was completing her fellowship was sent to do the procedure. She requested that we meet her down in the radiology room since the X-Ray Department had allowed the quick procedure to take place. The female surgeon explained that she would make a small incision in Sierra's neck to remove the shunt. A nurse accompanied Sierra and I down to the main floor and Sierra was placed on a padded table and was promptly connected to a cardiac rate monitor and the oxymeter.

The surgeon did not put Sierra under anesthetic. I thought she would give Sierra a local to numb the area, but the procedure began as soon as she was hooked up to the machines. The surgeon passed me the tubing with the oxygen mask and asked me to hold it to supplement Sierra throughout the procedure.

The glint of the metal scalpel flashed quickly as the surgeon made a two centimeter long incision on my daughter's tender neck. I tried to speak to Sierra in a soothing voice as she screamed loudly. Blood trickled down her soft little neck as the surgeon located the carotid artery. The procedure the surgeon believed would be only a few seconds developed into minutes of minor surgery as the discovery of not just a shunt but also two metal staples and two black nylon souchers was made. The surgeon cursed loudly as she pulled at the staple only to lose the grip. On the monitor I watched in horror as Sierra's heart rate climbed steeply towards 200 beats per minute. I held the oxygen mask closer and tried to soothe her with my voice, but she was enduring a surgical procedure without any anesthetic and the tiny metal tweezers now dug at the tender flesh of her neck. She screamed more frantically as the first staple was removed and I could clearly see the mass of the carotid artery which looked like a rigid pink straw in her neck. The surgeon got a firm grip on the black nylon soucher which had gradually been working its way to the surface, and it was removed. I glanced at the monitor and saw Sierra's heart rate crest well above 220 beats and I loudly screamed for the surgeon to stop. The woman looked at me and then at the monitor and the brutal gouging of my daughter's neck came to an abrupt halt.

I stood shaking as gauze, antibiotic ointment and tape were quickly placed over the incision site. Sierra's nurse bundled her up in blankets and carried her out of radiology into a side post operative recovery room, where Sierra's heart rate was continuously monitored. The nurse immediately gave Sierra pain medication and I cradled her softly around tubes and wires, speaking soothing words in her little ears as she cried and cried.

The nurse refused to take Sierra back upstairs to the pediatric ward until she was sure Sierra's heart rate was stable and dropping to below 200 beats per minute. We spoke about the unbelievable procedure we had just witnessed. The nurse and I could not believe a local anesthetic had not been given for the sake of "saving time". The nurse asked me why I hadn't demanded that the process be stopped sooner. I meekly explained that in the Special Care Nursery, I had witnessed Sierra undergo similar distressing events and on some level, I had grown accustomed to seeing her endure a great deal of stress. What I had not considered was that even when Sierra was experiencing those procedures in the SCN, she was on high levels of morphine and other pain medication through IVs. The procedure my daughter had just endured most people would never even do to an animal.

The young nurse, Abbey, did everything she could to calm Sierra and gave her as much pain medication as was possible to help my little girl. Eventually, after 30 long, excruciating minutes, Sierra's heart rate began a steady decent below 200 beats per minute. The nurse and I breathed a heavy sigh of relief. Double wrapped in warm blue blankets, we carried Sierra carefully into the elevator and back up to the pediatric ward. Abbey ensured Sierra was as comfortable and settled as possible and that all of her apparatus was connected, then she went to the nursing station to debrief the shocking incident with the head nurse.

A formal complaint was made and the details of the incident were reviewed by the hospital authorities. The surgeon was informally reprimanded and the matter was dropped, but how an event like that could have occurred still boggles my mind.

Chapter 8

The single biggest problem
in communication
is the illusion
that it has taken place.

~ George Bernard Shaw

Sierra was again flown back to Kelowna after her fundal placation surgery was abruptly cancelled. I felt like every fiber of my being was shattering. It was so tempting to just stare out a window and be non-responsive; to give in to a snuggly apathy that would cushion my mind, enveloping me from reality.

I had to consciously snap my attention back to the scene at hand, forcing myself to repeat the monotonous hospital routine over and over.

It was becoming harder to find inspiration or hope in my surroundings. The beige and non-descript "only in hospitals" green suffocated my spirit more and more. Sierra's shiny little eyes were the only light I saw some days, and I have come to believe that in many ways, she was the one helping me heal, not the other way around.

Nurses again set us up in a private room to ensure limited viral evils would slip into our space. I began daring them. I would literally will another curve ball to be thrown at me so I could take my anger and revenge out on something new. Any feeling would be better than this idle waiting in suspended time.

The same pediatrician handled Sierra's case and a familiarity that comes with daily interaction and decreased inhibition due to exhaustion crept into our dialogue. I could identify which nurse or doctor was about to enter our room just from the echoing footstep rhythm in the hall. I knew the custodian who would sweep and mop the beige melamine floor. The mundane rituals of scheduled hospital routine silently ebbed at my mind, draining me of any life force.

We settled in to what would become close to another month of waiting. The pediatricians at Children's Hospital had said that Sierra could go home on the nasal jejunum tube and oxygen with me acting as nurse. This gave me the inspiration I needed to resume my fight. I began to focus on getting prepared to bring my daughter home.

The issue of Sierra going home was not as cut and dry as I had initially believed. Our pediatrician was very hesitant to give the okay for Sierra to be cared for at home. However, the medical team in Vancouver had said she was able to be cared for at home with integrated agency support. The transition to our own house would require community support staff to provide equipment and training for me to effectively provide Sierra's care. They would also have to closely monitor Sierra's progress each week.

Our pediatrician was more comfortable letting Sierra go home once she had a permanent mic-key tube inserted into her stomach which would occur during the fundal placation operation. Children's Hospital felt that she was more than ready to go home, as they send home children on this nasal feeding tube all the time; granted, many of the children may not have the respiratory complications that Sierra did. Mark and I were beyond ready to take our child home, as we were approaching 130 days in the hospital. The issues governing the decision were deeply clouded. It was disconcerting to realize that these choices about our daughter's life were not ours to make. An entire medical community had to be consulted before any decision about living circumstances could occur. The degree of powerlessness and dependency one experiences in these situations is too often overlooked. Resentment and fear mounted as our daughter's transfer home became a paper shuffle and telephone tag game reminiscent of a chess game. "My Children's Hospital knight takes your Kelowna General rook."

When it seemed that our current pediatrician was not in favour of permitting Sierra to go home, Mark called our neonatologist , Dr. Singh, in Vancouver and calmly stated the hurdles we were facing and the fact that the pediatrician in Vancouver had said she could be cared for at home. Mark and Doctor Singh had formed a type of bond at Children's that I can only describe as "Boys Club". While on ECMO with many silent hours to talk, Mark discovered that the Head of the ECMO Team had gone to the rival University of Queens at the same time Mark was doing his Masters at Western in what is now coined Kinesiology. Dr. Singh had joined in on the conversation as they shared stories of team rivalries and old hangouts. Now, Dr. Singh listened intently to Mark as he explained our predicament and frustration and he insisted that he would look into things on his end.

This move did not impress our pediatrician, but we were no longer in the mood for niceties. To us, it felt as if our daughter was being held hostage. Dr. Singh contacted our local Hospital and the Head Pediatrician at Children's and it was confirmed that Sierra Robinson was indeed ready to make the move home, before the fundal placation surgery and the transfer process should begin.

Our pediatrician made it clear she was acting on the advice of Children's Hospital and did not feel this was necessarily the best move for Sierra. She implied she didn't think I was capable of caring for Sierra at home. Maintaining the tiny shreds of calm I still had, I explained that I had already cared for one baby and knew all of Sierra's equipment inside and out, and had been administering many of the feeds myself. She insisted there was still a lot to learn and I would need to be doing it all myself throughout the night and day. She threw at me a statement saying I seemed to have not been coping just being in the hospital.

Breathing deeply, I again quietly explained that being in the hospital was a stress unto itself, and if anything, I would be in my own home with both my children, not volleying between the two of them insufficiently as I was now.

Things finally began to happen, but like political undercurrents, bureaucracy too has infected every hospital corridor. Aligning the necessary players to do the training became a feat unto itself. Equipment had to be ordered through the At Home Program which meant sitting and waiting while countless forms and phone calls were completed, through various government agencies. To get an IV pole to go home, it took eight days. Each morning I saw idle batches of them in the halls and my patience sloughed further away.

A close friend of mine who I knew from work had kept in close daily contact with me while I had been in Vancouver at the beginning of Sierra's ordeal. Although she had still never met Sierra, she had seen pictures and received daily updates of Sierra's progress, or steps backwards, as had been the case many a day. Her own son, in his twenties, had been a patient at Children's Hospital for most of his life as he was dealing with a degenerative disorder and mental challenges. Joan was no stranger to this world and her experience and wisdom helped me in ways she may never know. Now that we were in Kelowna, she was able to come down to visit us, and see firsthand how Sierra was progressing.

Joan entered the room with her quiet smile and I think I flung my exhaustion directly into her tiny body. I hugged her with a fierceness that surprised me, for there had been so many nights when I had spoken to her and truly thought she would never get the experience of seeing my child alive. She held me up and I saw little tears in her eyes as she glanced at Sierra.

"Oh, Michelle! She's doing so well. She's beautiful." Joan smiled broadly as she approached her.

"I know," I whispered. "I know."

We chatted frantically, trying to fit in every missed visit into the half hour slot and I glanced disappointedly at the intruder when the nurse walked in to give me infant first aid training. She asked if Joan would like to stay and take part and Joan replied, "What the heck!"

We were each handed the plastic baby to practice breathing and CPR and to learn the Heimlich maneuver. It was good to have someone with a light heart to do the training with as I was usually neck deep in serious conversation or silence. Bright sunlight shone into the room as the nurse gave us detailed directions for each stage of the training and we took turns with the doll in vain attempts to bring it back to life. For the choking training, we were to check in the baby's mouth then flip it over and with the heel of our hand, briskly bang the baby's back midway up with a forward motion. Joan did an excellent job with her baby. Passing it to me, I checked the baby's mouth then flipped it over and banged as instructed on the doll's back. The baby's head slammed violently into the table in front of me and Joan and I burst into wild fits of laughter I can still hear.

"Looks like your baby isn't going to make it!" Joan laughed and I doubled over with wracking sobs of hysteria. I couldn't remember the last time I had laughed and I swam through each wave of giggles like body surfing on warm swells of salty ocean.

The nurse looked at us with serious disapproval, but I couldn't stop my laughing fit and it only got worse each time I glanced at Joan. I felt as if I was thirteen, giggling loudly intensifying each time I looked at Joan or the glassy eyed doll who would have had a major concussion or broken neck. I thought the nurse was going to send me out into the hall.

Eventually, our laughter subsided enough that the nurse could proceed with the instruction, but each time I looked at Joan's mischievous eyes, we would start laughing again. The nurse couldn't wait to complete the session and pack up. Somehow, I got certified.

I think about eight days had passed since we had heard Sierra could go home, and each morning I would arrive earlier to check with the front desk to see if today would be the day. Each morning I was greeted with the same reply.

"We have no release forms here. Are you sure it was going to be today?"

Frustration and anger grew by the hour. It was unclear as to what the hold-up was and when we asked the nursing administrator for information she would explain that we were waiting for equipment orders to go through or responses from the At Home Program. We then hit a weekend and another two days of office inactivity impeded any progress to going home.

The following Tuesday, I was sure things would finally be organized and when I checked in again with the head nurse, I was told that things were progressing as quickly as they could and just to be patient.

I drove home to tell Mark. He had planned on coming in later, fully expecting that we would be loading the car with equipment and finally strapping our child into her infant carrier. When I told him that things were still not organized, he had finally had enough and he charged into the house to the phone to speak with the nursing administrator.

I sat deflated beside Sierra's empty crib in her room, just wishing we could be bringing her here.

Mark is very talented at stating his point and he has a charismatic demeanor which usually serves him well, however, he was neither being charismatic nor patient as he spoke with the nursing administrator in the hall. I overheard some of the call.

"We have been waiting for over eight days for your people to get this organized. She has been in the hospital for over four and a half months. Children's Hospital has given the go ahead for her to come home. We are taking Sierra home today with whatever equipment is available!"

He hung up the phone fuming and I decided to drive back in on my own and see exactly what else needed to be done. Mark said he would follow in a few hours with the truck.

When I got to Sierra's room, I was greeted by the social worker who had been assigned to our case. Yes, you get a social worker who is suppose to gently assess finances and judge whether you are eligible for financial aid or counseling throughout the crisis. I have never been one for talking to a complete stranger about my inner most feelings and felt this to be an intrusion more than an offering of help.

On this day, the young male in his mid thirties followed me in to Sierra's room and pulled up the green straight backed chair stating that he needed to talk to me. I put my things down and focused on Sierra who was glancing around the room silently at her hanging toys.

"So, how are you doing, Michelle?" His syrupy voice slid across the room, too sticky for my liking.

"I'm good." I replied without adding anything extra, the meat for which he was in such evident need.

"I heard Sierra is going home soon."

My wheels started turning. I worked in a system very similar to this and began to resent its very existence.

"You must be getting frustrated, having to wait for Sierra to go home."

He was cutting too close to the bone and my throat began to tighten in the way I despise.

I gave him enough to appease. "Yes, it is frustrating. We would like her home."

He inched forward in his chair, his practiced look of sympathy moving his pale brow. "How are things at home?"

My skin prickled and my eyes darted in challenge to meet his. So this is what you are here for, I silently declared. No you don't.

"Things are fine."

"I understand Mark is getting frustrated with the situation too." *Social worker-ese* meant to do its magic.

I simply nodded as my throat continued to tighten despite my willing it to relax. I breathed, but to no avail.

"Do you and Mark ever fight?"

Do ducks like water? I had a hard time keeping the sneer from forming on my top lip.

"Sometimes. I think all married couples do." I replied quickly.

"Does Mark ever get aggressive?"

On cue, in walked our pediatrician.

"No, he doesn't." I stated, wishing my response had sounded more forceful. Swirling rage was rising too quickly inside me and I knew if it escaped, my daughter might not be coming home. This was spiraling into something much bigger than I had anticipated.

I continued, "I don't appreciate what you are insinuating about my marriage. Things are fine. We have been under a tremendous amount of stress and anyone would be fed up by this point."

Our pediatrician said her piece. " Mark made a phone call earlier threatening to take Sierra out of the hospital whether we had the forms signed or not. His call greatly disturbed our Nursing Administrator. He seems to have quite a temper." She paused, hoping for clarification.

My throat betrayed me and closed completely. Tears started coursing down my cheeks. It took every bit of strength to remain calm.

"We are both very frustrated." I said softly between sobs, hating myself for portraying a weak female, much to the chagrin of the two standing before me. I could see the pediatrician chalking this up to her character assessment of me not being able to cope.

"Mark and I have been doing this for over four and a half months. Children's Hospital said almost two weeks ago that Sierra can go home. We want her home. Why is everything taking so long?" My voice came out whiney and fragile.

"It takes a while to get everything in place." The counselor said, more fake syrup dripping off his spliced tongue.

I steadied myself, realizing this impromptu interview might be a determining factor in whether I was capable of caring for my daughter in the pediatrician's eyes.

"We are ready to have Sierra home. Mark is angry at the amount of time it is taking to get things organized. He would never take Sierra from the hospital unless she was ready and we had all of her necessary equipment."

"That's not what it sounded like when he phoned earlier." The doctor said with a condescending tone. "He could be making a grave mistake if he plans to follow through on what he said. We would have to involve security."

"This could not be a scene from my life", I thought to myself, the rapid dizzying events tumbled around like rough edged stones.

"Mark needs to calm down before we progress any further. You need to tell him to stop threatening to take Sierra."

I looked at her debating what the right look or thing to say would be to end this ridiculous discourse. I chose meekness.

"I will. It won't happen again."

"We are doing everything we can. You both need to be patient."

The doctor turned abruptly and left.

The counselor looked at me again. "You are sure there is nothing you want to talk to me about."

I spat it," Would you like to tell me about your marriage?"

He was taken aback. Part of me was shocked, but the stronger part was coming out swinging, ready with more.

I finally responded, "There isn't anything to tell. Things are fine. We are just frustrated."

That seemed to satiate him and question period was over. He picked up his bag and quickly left the room, no doubt to consult with the nursing team and our pediatrician. I felt like I was living under a powerful microscope, only people were choosing how to interpret what they saw to solidify their own beliefs. It wasn't accurate and it wasn't in the best interest of the family.

Politics are everywhere. I am such an optimist and some would say naïve, but I wish there could be some pristine facets of our world which were unstained. Personal goals and ideals all too often impede us from making the necessary choices to further our progress as a race and at times it stirs in me sadness so deep I feel ill.

Again, I reached for Sierra for solace. She had remained quiet and relaxed throughout the whole conflict. I traced my fingers up and down her little arm. She looked at me with the purist eyes and I wondered how we had created a society so barren and how each adult individual had lost every tattered shred of innocence and trust with which we entered this world.

Attitude keeps me going
or cripples my progress.
It alone fuels my fire
or assaults my hope.
No barrier too high,
no valley too deep,
no dream too extreme
and no challenge too great.

~ Charles Swindoll

Chapter 9

Sun illuminated the delicate chartreuse leaves moving in rhythmic silence in the wind. I sat mesmerized by the movement, a gentle dance between wind and limb, nurturing the sap inside to flow.

The tentative start of spring was merging into a bountiful summer mode. Lush grass cushioned my bare feet as I walked briskly to refill the bird feeder and survey the yard. We are fortunate to live above Okanagan Lake, and our home is tenderly flanked by tall ponderosa pines that tower above the house.

I had spent hours and hours each year gardening and moving stones to create flower beds and little pathways through the trees in anticipation of having children to run through them as they played tag. The vision was so crisp, at times I could hear their laughter escape the dirt as I turned each clump of grey earth.

It was so obvious our family was in crisis. Our little yard had shriveled to a burnt out husk of dead leaves and twigs. Flowers that would have usually been in full bloom lay dormant in crispy buds starved of water and care. It was amazing to me to view this, detached as I was from my usual life. Our home had shrunk to a basic nucleus in an effort to survive. Any superfluous extension had been deprived to focus all energy and essentials to the survival of the core.

From a distance, one would have thought the care taker of this land had died. In a manner of speaking, part of me had.

Our pediatrician did an excellent job of explaining in detail the reams of equipment and medications Sierra would require. Sierra would need a crib fitted with a specialized raised mattress to keep her at a sharp angle to help with the reflux. Mark quickly constructed a plywood base at a 30° angle to support Sierra's tiny frame which would fit on her mattress. We planned to get some foam to use as a cushion.

On a crisp Tuesday morning, Mark was setting up his display for the opening of his store when an unknown man walked in to make an inquiry.

He simply began, "I've never been in before, but my wife has and she's doing some spring cleaning."

Mark gave the man a knowing nod and smirk, communicating understanding of wifely ways and wishes.

"She suggested I bring something in to see if you had any use for it. You build custom furniture, right?"

Mark smiled and answered, "I do. What is it you have?"

"Well, it's been in our basement for a while, and she thought it might be useful. It is some angled foam, but I don't think it will be of much use."

Mark's eyes fixed on the man's face. He smiled and leaned against the front desk. "Did Ted send you in?" Ted was a close friend of ours who knew our situation well, but the man shook his head.

"No, I don't know a Ted."

Mark named off a few more people who knew of our plight.

The man furrowed his brow in confusion. "Well, I don't know any of those people. My wife just thought of your store, thinking you could use this. I understand if you can't. We were just cleaning out the house."

Mark stood silently in disbelief, then, he quietly explained his bewilderment to the stranger. "Our baby has been in the hospital for almost 5 months and she is coming home for the first time later this week. She has severe respiratory issues and is constantly vomiting and dealing with reflux. The doctors said we need a special raised bed for her. I just constructed a wooden form last night to put in her crib and we needed to get some foam to place on top. I was going to buy some this afternoon on the way home."

The man stared at Mark as the depth of their serendipitous encounter sank in further. "This foam sounds like just what you need."

There was a long moment as Mark stared at him incredulously and nodded. The unknown man brought in the slanted 30° foam. Mark thanked him and they shared one last bewildered glance before parting.

Sierra's room was initially shared with Daniel, but we fitted it with an odd assortment of medical equipment and apparatus necessary for her care. We place a large black hook on the wall just to the side of her crib to suspend the sterile feeding bag. The tube would go from the bag to Sierra's face where it was taped securely into her nose.

On the window sill, we placed her oxymeter, to monitor her blood oxygen and beside it, the suction machine that had been sent by the Red Cross Society. Oxygen tanks lay leaning against the wall and little boxes and containers held her bandages. New catheter tubing, guaze and medical tape for her face to hold the oxygen tubes and feeding tubes in place were carefully stacked. Distilled water and syringes for flushing her line were in waiting. Small medical scissors and antibiotic ointment for her incision site on her neck sat strategically on a suspended shelf for quick access.

During her first few months home, Daniel was ousted from his room and I slept on his bed, to monitor Sierra and tend to her during the night. She needed to be fed every three to four hours via the feeding pump and I was still pumping milk for her which we froze and thawed for the feeds. The oxygen tank rested against the wall and the tubing was held in place under her blankets and mattress. It was surreal having her home. The insane rushing between the house and the hospital abruptly ceased. We were still going for hospital visits every three or four days for Sierra to receive shots, weighing or assessments, but she was home, finally, in our house.

Her care was continuous and intense. I would jump up out of a dead sleep in the night from the bed to the side of the crib when I heard the first sounds of her throwing up. I don't know enough about how the mind works, but I would immediately wake at the first slight abnormal gurgle, knowing it was life or death for Sierra if she inhaled any of the regurgitated bolus of food slowly dripping into her through-out the night. I would stop the machine and flip her quickly so any vomit would dribble out of her mouth onto the bed and not down her trachea.

I would be sterilizing feeding equipment and tubing at 2 am and reloading the feeding pump, setting it to her precise feeds of 46ml per hour. I would then sit on the couch in virtual darkness hooked up to the breast pump to extract the milk which would eventually be poured into the plastic bag and drip slowly through the tubes down her nose and esophagus into her jejunum. Everything was scientific and precise, based on continued hospital scheduling and measurements calibrated to her needs and planned weight gain for the upcoming operation.

She was on a medicine schedule that I typed up for reference. Some meds were every three hours, some every four and some every twelve. We had boxes of syringes and I would prepare them in advance for the day, setting up meds for hours later in the fridge as I had seen the nurses do in the hospital. This ensured accurate measurement in the middle of the night, as each medication lay in wait in the fridge. A fine tuned routine evolved, with each moment composed and notated like orchestrated music.

My three year old would float between my consciousness in brief waves of inactivity, becoming my right hand when Sierra started to vomit uncontrollably. He knew how to run for a cloth, which button was pause on her feeding machine, and how to help hold Sierra's hands above her head as she cried while I frantically re-taped the dislodged feeding tube she had pulled from her face to avoid a visit to the radi-ologist for re-insertion.

He knew not to touch her flashing equipment with the pretty coloured lights in her room, no matter how enticing. Daniel became extremely well versed in medical language even as he was still acquir-ing basic English. He played in the spaces void of Sierra's medical entourage and learned to co-exist with a high needs sibling. He was still such a little boy.

During the first days of "home-integration" a team of 5 medical professionals arrived at my door in separate vehicles, all with specific mandates to carry out in terms of Sierra's ongoing care. There was the respiratory therapist who set up all oxygen equipment and reviewed all aspects of the oxymeter monitoring with me. The Community nurse was there to do basic weighing and immunization needs and to familiarize herself with the newest high risk infant on her case load. The occupational therapist arrived with reams of exercises we needed to perform daily to ensure Sierra's muscles began to develop in an effort to strengthen her core and large muscle groups. She could not go on her stomach because it put too much pressure on her lungs and diaphragm and restricted her oxygen intake. She also instructed me in methods to begin reducing the oral aversion Sierra had ingrained out of sheer survival reflex.

The At Home Program Coordinator was there to ensure that all equipment was operational and that I had received sufficient training. A respite nurse was there to ensure that twice a week I would have three hours to spend with my son. My head spun as each player claimed a stake in my children's world. The fish bowl existence continued.

Sierra's next abdominal operation was finally confirmed at Children's Hospital for July 23rd. We traveled down for assessment and preparation on the 20th, now old pros at the procedure. Sierra was about to undergo her fourth surgery and was not yet 6 months old. This operation would repair the entrance of the stomach to help curb her uncontrolled vomiting which was occurring at an alarming rate of up to 13 times a day. It was vital that it was successful to ensure she could digest food orally and not be at constant risk for aspiration or malnutrition. They would place the feeding tube through a hole into her stomach, which would be held in place by an inflatable balloon. The next phase of our existence was beginning to unfold.

You don`t drown by falling in water,
You drown by staying there.

~ Unknown

Chapter 10

Our shoulders slumped heavily as Sierra was finally sedated and wheeled on the gurney into the depths of the OR corridors. Heavy metal doors closed mechanically in front of us, barring our entry. Mark and I stood bereft of thought for just a moment, as our daughter's life was once again placed in the hands of others with sterile knives, intricate technology and chemical concoctions which knotted our tongues.

The familiar bitter bile began to gather at the back of my throat and I finally breathed, releasing tight clenched fists. We moved silently, politely, back to the fluorescent lit waiting room, typically complete with eight sets of anxious faces awaiting the outcome of other children.

I hate magazines. The glossy, lipstic clad, botoxed, and starving carcasses stared blankly at us all. The issues screamed with the ludicrous state of our society: How to buy more for less, how to create an organized luxury bathroom, how to multi-task to live a faster life and of course, how to lose ridiculous amounts of weight. As a former bulimic, I always scan that one; a perfection driven nature can be hell for a teen striving for some control.

Quantum physics talks of the causal effect, stating that "there are not really two categories of things in the world: objects and processes, there are only relatively fast processes and relatively slow processes." It determines that nothing actually is except "in a very approximate and temporary sense. How something is or what state it is, is but an illusion."

I became a textbook study in the causal relationship of intense levels of stress and drive. I entered university a year early and took 6 courses a semester, including Latin at my mother's insistence. At 19,

I enrolled in a third year physiological psychology course. Leaving a lecture one evening as I carried my books for my six courses, I froze in mid-step on the tile riser, staring blankly at the brick walls around me. I froze in time, watching with an eerie detachment as young adults streamed past me in self-absorbed waves.

I was terrified. I had actually forgotten what I was doing. I finally remembered that I was in mid-step and should continue walking down the stairs, but a silent fear me gripped me and I finally succumbed.

Working at two jobs, and my stress from an overloaded course load in a mission to enter teaching and architecture, toppled me in one swift blow.

I sat on my doctor's metal, foam padded, paper covered table and told him carefully measured bits of my behaviours that concerned me. No one would be aware of my secret trick to stay skinny and acceptable. Friends attributed my slight build to my running and swimming; this façade would continue at all costs.

I shared my fear regarding freezing on the steps, my stress and frustration of perpetually arguing with my mother, my long standing, leading role as mediator between my parents for the past 7 years and the fact that their long-overdue divorce was unveiling as we spoke. I told him some of my crazy schedule and I mentioned the third year course I had been taking. He swiftly explained the seriousness of the situation and how I needed to reduce my stress levels, then he essentially ordered me to finally leave my mother's house. I took his advice.

The day I moved out, my mother and I yelled at each other up until the moment I stepped out the threshold with my final box. She demanded back my house key as, "this was no longer my home." I rolled my eyes and I'm sure spat something suitably insulting and climbed immediately into my red Honda civic, slamming the door and peeling away for punctuation.

Tears eventually cascaded, but I suppressed them momentarily, in the ever increasing black hole of my solar plexus. The sickening burn there lingered as a constant ebb for days. I was more determined than ever to maintain the sense of illusion, not allowing myself time to realize how devouring my life had become.

Now, sitting in Vancouver in the OR waiting room as surgeons souchered the top of my daughter's stomach in an effort to create a way for her to keep down nourishment, I once again silently promised to cherish my health as I truly believed this element of Sierra's condition was inflicted as karma. So ironic it was that my baby was doomed to tube feeding because she could not keep down food.

To see things in the seed,
that is genius.

~ Lao Tzu

Chapter 11

Is spirituality and intuition the antimatter to scientific research and quantum physics? Why are the leading researchers in the field of quantum theory so fearful when it results in a sense of mysticism?

As a child laying awake in the dark on hot, clammy summer nights, sheets sopping wet under my slight weight with perspiration, I would absentmindedly rub my index finger and thumb together in concentric circles with my eyes closed and my consciousness would delve to each end of the spectrum. The same motion would elicit thoughts of the largest thing imaginable then flip to the most infinitesimally small object I could fathom. Over and over, I would observe as my mind swam from one immense sensation to the opposing pole and gradually, I would be lulled into a foggy slumber.

The only object which I could associate with this experience was a milky white plastic cup we had in our laminate kitchen cupboard. On the front was an image of a monkey holding the same cup with an image of another smaller monkey holding the exact cup with an image of an even smaller monkey holding a cup…this was my first glimpse of the concept of infinity; I was five.

Mark and I spoke with the kids often about the scientific aspect of the anatomy of the human body. We have done so since we brought Sierra home and attempted to explain to three year old Daniel what each machine did for Sierra and what each procedure attempted to correct. We used the full scientific names from the onset. When we discussed her reflux, we said, "the food is coming back up the esophagus" and stressed the importance of it not going down into her "trachea."

Frequent visits to the library always allowed Daniel chances to choose piles of his own books and I would augment his selection with illustrated children's books of the human body. He had so many questions at the age of four and five about her lungs, how the heart worked, what happened in her digestive tract with the "tummy-tube". He clearly wanted to understand the need for procedures or X-rays that would once again pre-occupy his mother, the abstract concept of Vancouver eventually stealing her for days.

Sierra always sat with us as we poured over the books. One advantage to Sierra's oral aversion meant Daniel's books did not have to suffer the traditional baby gumming of each paper page or the cardboard corners of covers going soggy. She never put anything in her mouth.

She would touch the pages and Daniel and I would have ridiculously in depth conversations about what happened to the blood that seeped back through the ventrical septal defect into the wrong chamber of her heart where it didn't get oxygen. My brief training in Montessori Methodology reinforced that there was never too early a time to introduce complex concepts to a child. It encouraged following a child's curiosity, as they would take from each experience what they were ready for, as a type of background knowledge that would lay dormant but waiting in the intricate neurological webbing of the brain, waiting to be activated years later.

Daniel's natural curiosity and my insatiable need to understand the physiology of the birth defect became a primary bonding experience as we logged hours over those books. It was the rare time Sierra faded from my focus as he and I talked and looked and questioned.

As Daniel grew, we continued with more detailed graphics, using computer enhanced images to peer into the body's inner organs. At the age of 2½, Sierra surprised us with her level of anatomical knowledge and vocab. How did I not realize that she would of course absorb it all as well?

As human beings, our greatness lies
not so much in being able to remake the world
as in being able to remake ourselves.

~ Gandhi

Chapter 12

By August 1st of 2003, Sierra had recovered enough from the surgery to be brought home. Mark was already back at home and I was in Vancouver with Daniel, my Mom, Grandma and Sierra in the hospital. The morning they released her, complete with the new tummy tube. I was elated as my child's face was almost bereft of tubes.

The yellow plastic tubing that had resided in one nasal passage way for feeds was finally gone, and Sierra seemed relieved as well.

The "mic-key" feeding tube which went through a small hole the surgeons had cut into Sierra's stomach, had a little cap that could be closed or opened, depending on whether Sierra was hooked up to food.

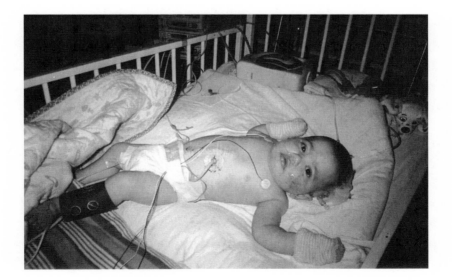

She still had the "kangaroo pump", an ingenious device which I usually carried over my shoulder. It was a heavy blue canvas material with flaps that opened to reveal the operating feeding pump and the level of food still left in the plastic feeding bag. It was connected via yet another tube to Sierra's mic-key and went straight into the stomach, bypassing any oral or esophageal entry. It allowed us to be mobile during the day. The site around the stomach opening was still very fresh and sore and needed to be cleaned and sterilized thoroughly during healing.

The top of Sierra's abnormally shaped stomach had been stitched to reduce the size of the opening where the esophagus was attached. This internal fix was supposed to reduce the frequency and severity of the involuntary regurgitation of all of her food. So far, so good.

That same morning, I would begin the process of moving out of Dennis' basement suite. For seven full months, he had allowed us to invade his home, at times with extended family, in order to navigate the ordeal. Finally, I could give him back his home which he had so generously opened to us all.

I brought Sierra out of the ward in her car seat carrier and soon arrived at the doorway of Children's, where I met Dr. Singh. He stopped to wish us well and encouraged us to keep him posted on her progress and needs. This man seemed more like a father than our doctor, and it was all I could do not to hug him. I waved good-bye and triumphantly exited the building with my six month old at my side.

When I arrived at the basement suite, I had hoped the packing process would be well under way, but my mother and my 89 year old Grandmother were busy enough just keeping up with Daniel. It was a crazy three hours as I hastily packed up and tidied the suite. I scrubbed out the fridge as I placed a lunch of sorts in front of my son. My mom was in some sort of trance, watching as movement happened around her. For about 20 minutes, Sierra cried in her carrier and my mother looked on in confusion. I had to eventually tell her to rock Sierra so I could continue the moving out process. At some level, I think she feared holding Sierra, as she was unsure what would hurt this fragile creature. I had grown so acclimatized to Sierra's unique entourage of equipment, that I barely gave her fragile status a second thought.

Finally, the basement suite was empty and my vehicle was packed with everyone's belongings. Daniel was loaded in beside my mother, Sierra was facing backward in her little car seat and the feeding pack and oxygen tank were positioned so I could easily reach them from the driver's side. I helped my grandmother negotiate the staircase to get up to the front of the yard and buckled her in too. I was exhausted, and I still had to take them out to the ferry terminal then start my 5 hour trek to Kelowna with my two children in tow.

I said goodbye and thanked my mother and grandmother for all of their support, as they had uprooted their lives yet again to look after Daniel while I tended to Sierra in the hospital. They boarded the ferry for Victoria and I hooked up Sierra's feeding tube and checked the oxygen rate and tubing one last time before sliding into the front seat and beginning the drive home.

In all of the confusion, I had apparently misunderstood Mark when we spoke that morning about the details of the trip. I thought he had said he would meet us in Merrit, to take Daniel with him and help accompany us home. After three hours of driving, frequently stopping to get food for Daniel or to check Sierra's kangaroo pump, we arrived at Merrit close to 7:00pm. I stopped to phone Mark to see where he was, but received no answer at home, so I figured he was on his way. I took out Sierra and Daniel and I walked around for a bit, to stretch and get some fresh air. Daniel's curiousity led him to finding all sorts of treasures, even in the small parking lot and rest area. He found striped stones, interesting bugs and a barrier which he turned into a jungle gym of sorts.

After about an hour, I phoned Mark again, and still got no answer. Daniel was complaining of being hungry again and Sierra would cry off and on. I still had doses of medicine with codeine to give her to help ease the pain of the operation site and I administered another pre-measured syringed dose directly into the hole in her stomach. Fresh red blood and liquid seeped out one side of the incision site, and I dabbed it carefully with gauze and the sterilized wipes I had been given. Soon our waiting turned into close to two hours and I decided to continue driving, not knowing where Mark could be, but wanting to get moving before it got too dark.

I drove down the road, looking for his vehicle, wondering if something had happened. Neither of us had cell phones at the time. I drove about a half hour out, then thought maybe I should go back to Merrit to phone some friends of ours to see if they knew what had happened. No one knew where Mark was and I phoned home one last time to check our messages in case he left one for me there. When I phoned he answered. It was now going for 10:00.

"Where are you?" I blurted, a new silent anger beginning to develop in my gut.

"I was waiting for you to come home. Where are you?"

"We are in Merrit. We have been for the past 2 hours. I thought you were going to meet us here." My voice was rising sharply. Sierra began crying softly in the car.

"I don't see the point of me driving out there at this time of night. Just head on home."

I was so frustrated. "We have been waiting at this rest stop for you to arrive! Daniel is hungry! Sierra's stomach is oozing blood mixed with light coloured puss! I had to completely move out of Dennis' by myself!"

"You weren't by yourself. What about your Mom and Grandma?"

I silently shook my head in disbelief. I quickly said that I was on my way and fumed as I entered the dark vehicle. Fortunately, as we drove the last hour and a half home, Daniel and Sierra quickly fell asleep so I could focus solely on my situation. How could he have left me to do all of this on my own? How could he not even apologize for not following through to meet us? When I tried to convey my fear about the ooze seeping from Sierra, he just muttered, "that's normal after an operation", yet it wasn't his eyes taking in the obscenity of the hole and the apparatus gouged into my child's abdomen. By the time I reached our home, it was close to midnight.

The front door light flicked on as he heard the vehicle enter the top of the driveway. Mark emerged to come get Daniel from the car. I scowled and stated how inconsiderate he was to us all, and he answered that I better get some rest to get myself under control. Between trips of carrying children and luggage out of the car, he and I bickered as he backtracked and said he had never agreed to meet me in Merrit; that he was waiting to hear from me.

"Didn't you get all of the messages I left?" I yelled into the darkness.

"I was out and didn't get home until 9:00, then there was no point in heading out."

I stared at him then broke into sobs as the weight of all of the stress finally descended full bore. Mark responded saying how ridiculous I was becoming, but I had no anger left to retort. I just cried and descended into quiet apathy.

I finished unloading the car under the clear, star streaked night and realized the depth of my aloneness with this task. It seemed Mark was not concerned about my well being. He only cared that I continue to meet all of the medical and other essential necessities of his children. In the darkness, it was clearly audible. An irreparable tear in the fabric of our marriage ripped through the silence that night; one I had no intention of ever trying to mend.

During my childhood, serendipity allowed me two years with an amazing woman at a time when I was beginning to become one myself.

Mrs. Knox was a beautiful woman, with blond shoulder length hair and a sense of humour that bordered on sarcasm drenched in love. Her skill at teaching was such a natural extension of her spirit and she energetically merged into each of our lives.

In grade five and six, I was a year younger than the rest of the students. Mrs. Knox would ensure we each gave our best effort in math, creative writing and art. She loved art. She helped us create a 5 foot mural made of square inch tiles of a school bus entering the yard with all of her students. Her creative, joie de vies showered over us all and for two years, I thrived under her care.

Mrs. Knox was diligent and used to write pointers to us in the margins of our writing books, sometimes correcting, but mostly suggesting how something could be improved or changed. Not being familiar with a teacher this thorough, I was taken aback by her surprise when she asked why I always commented back with my own remarks in the margin after receiving her insightful feedback. I thought that was what we were supposed to do.

In my comments, I would explain to her what I planned to change after reflecting on what she had said, or I would apologize for making so many spelling mistakes on the assignment, telling her my reason for rushing the night before. She would laugh openly at my remarks, but she smiled at me with a look that said, "continue."

It was Mrs. Knox who had the task of enlightening us with that first "sex-ed" talk, where the uncomfortable and purposefully overlooked discussion about our first menstruation was explicitly given to the eleven and twelve year old girls. It took me by complete surprise. There had never been any mention of this catastrophe by my mother. I remember silently shouting in disbelief, "Blood came from where?! Every month?", but I ensured that I kept my well practiced, ten year old, mature demeanor, so the other girls would not realize I had absolutely no clue.

One day in grade six, as I sat with a group of four girls who are still close friends, we giggled insistently about something and I was ostracized to isolation by moving my desk far from the group. I never got reprimanded at school and I felt a sickening shame at being moved. I remained in that spot for several days then it became the straw that broke me.

My Dad drank. He always had, but usually it was restricted to one or two rum and cokes which I had been taught to mix since the age of five. Two fingers for the rum after the cubes of ice, then coke would fill the glass. I would always sneak a sip of the coke.

Since our move to Peachland, his drinking took on a whole new meaning. Weekends became progressive excuses to disappear to the pub with his buddies, sometimes leaving Tammy and I outside to play at the park while he went in for a "quick visit". We didn't mind as we cherished the freedom of being on our own at the ages of 11 and 9 and we were just across the street from the store with the ice cream which he would ensure we had enough money to buy.

My Dad is a very interesting soul, smart intellectually and incredibly adept at meeting new people. He also has a strong wanderlust and loves to explore new places. He used to take my sister and I on long hikes in the mountains and we would have wonderful talks, as he sometimes shared stories from when he was a boy. Our five years in Peachland were magical for me in many ways, except for the fact that I was initiated into the role of confidant for my frequently drunk and pained father during the final three years.

My Dad would often come home late for dinner after spending the more and more frequent Saturday and Sunday afternoons at the pub. He would enter through the front door quietly and motion a hello by waving forward his hand and spreading his fingers in a method that communicated, "hi" and "not now" all at once.

I grew to learn how to become a silent observer, because I would need to know the nature of their quarrel later when my Dad chose to debrief and ask me to provide the reasons for my mother's distance. I would sit crouched on our open staircase, peering through the space between the stairs into the slim slice of dining room I could see. My father's dinner, after sitting on the table for well over an hour, would have been stashed into the oven to keep warm, but my mother's attitude was not.

My father would silently carry the plate to the table, his movements just off enough for me to gage the extent of his most recent alcohol infusion. He would ask my mom some standard,' just got home' questions and she would remark in curt phrases, bereft of elaboration, but gushing with the communiqué of the unsaid. In his state, my father would miss the cue of anger and frustration and continue on with his meal.

I would continue to crouch as the inevitable would occur. Some comment would unleash my mother's anger and the verbal battle would begin, complete with complaints, excuses and accusations which encompassed issues too deep to discuss here.

Long festering wounds would happily split open as fuel for the feud that continued before my eyes each weekend. Eventually, my father would get up, take a moment to steady himself, carefully put the finished plate on the counter beside the sink and make his way up to his room, as I frantically scampered away so as not to be caught listening. I would wait for his door to close, then, with measured thought, eventually enter his room to check the status of the sleeping giant. If he was already sleeping with a gentle snore, I would quietly exit again and close the door. If he was not asleep and sitting in the chair on the balcony, I would venture to the sliding door and poke my head out.

I would quietly open the heavy glass door and he would say, "Well, hi, Shelly-boo."

My heart strings would quiver as I drank in his state. Eventually, I would always implore, "Dad, why did you do this again."

"Do what?"

"Drink too much tonight." My voice would quietly question, but already I had begun the transformation into parent on the porch.

"Can't your old Dad have some fun with his friends on the weekend?"

At eleven, I began to get a quick education into having a conversation with someone who is inebriated.

"Of course you can have fun, Dad. But why do you always have to have too much."

"Those friends are some of the only ones who understand me. Your mother doesn't understand me."

A conversation which I never should have been part of was replayed over and over for years. "Dad, Mom cares about you, but she doesn't like it when you are like this."

"She won't even talk to me. She just talks to your grandma."

Ah! The joys of living in an extended family. I knew it all too well. Our entire family dynamic would change when my grandmother lived with us for up to six months out of the year. Sadly, I really didn't care much for her or appreciate her presence until I was sixteen. At the age of eleven, she seemed as disruptive as the gravitational pull of the moon set off course. My mother did confide in her, much to the detriment of all involved. Instead of taking issues that belonged between husband and wife, she would bring them to my grandmother and I would hear them hashed out in full on Jamaican dialect, the tone and rapidity of the syllables ever increasing with passion.

"Why he feel the need to go to them rumshop? Chu! He's a grown man!" My grandmother would state as only a Jamaican in heated discussion could.

For hours I would listen through the wall as they berated my father and my need to protect him became more and more deeply solidified. At least the months when my grandmother was not around, my mom had no one to berate him with and the feud would involve only the two individuals, not three.

Young children, while pure in vision, see situations only in black and white. They lack the knowledge of complexity to discern the adult world of layered greys ... but that is exactly their innocent beauty. Adult worlds are swirls of grey, truth layered with necessity, lies blended with kindness, restraint and patience slathered with smoldering passions and faded dreams. Is there value in grey?

Shadows are safe; suggestion enough for recognition, but hidden enough for protection. Adults cast beautifully crafted shadows of all shapes and sizes, but children peer closely into the cracks and crevices. They notice the details in their slowly emerging world.

You can't hide the truth from a child.

After school in Mrs. Knox's classroom, as she kept me afterschool that day, I told her I needed to move back with my friends and she asked if I could control my talking. I began to cry and she immediately knew this was no longer about our classroom situation. She must have held me for 5 minutes as I cried and cried, sopping the delicate pastel plaid pattern of her blouse. I remember our principal came in to speak with her about something, then realized the importance of the moment and quietly retracted from the room.

"What is going on?" She finally implored, gently moving me enough to look at me.

I sniffled loudly and shook my head. I couldn't say. I couldn't betray my family. On some level I think she knew.

I apologized for soaking her shirt and she said, "Well as long as you use a tissue instead of me, we're good." We laughed and her eyes attempted to quell the spouting well of my soul. "Are you going to be okay?"

I nodded and somehow, once again found the strength to resume my façade.

The following morning, she moved me back with my friends and time quietly souchered the revealed gash in my heart.

Chapter 13

Strange is our situation here on Earth.
Each of us comes for a short visit,
not knowing why,
yet some times seeming for a divine purpose.
There is one thing we do know:
that we are here for the sake of others...
for the countless unknown souls
whose fate we are connected to
by a bond of sympathy.

~ Albert Einstein

The bone protruded reprehensibly from her abdomen as I repositioned her for changing. Like a crooked finger it beckoned me to bend
and look closer. The lump was directly over the scarring from the diaphragmatic hernia repair doctor's had performed at two weeks of age,
but it seemed to have risen over night.

Now, at the age of 2 ½ , much had transpired in Sierra's world. She
was only on oxygen when grappling with a cold, she had been off her
feeding tube for several weeks, a feat that was astounding and which I
had battled for. Months and months of painstakingly stroking her face
with various textures to desensitize her oral aversion, charting how
many milliliters of milk she had taken orally each day before gagging
uncontrollably, and touching her tongue gently with various foods to

acquire a brief taste had paid off. My goal was to give Sierra the gift of eating orally without a tummy tube for her second birthday, and the two years of strategic, floundering attempts had proven effective.

Children's Hospital championed my efforts, but my local pediatrician seemed to doubt my determination every step of the way and warned that removing Sierra's feeding tube could prove detrimental.

Gradually, we actually had months of our life where we maintained some normalcy. Daniel was entering kindergarten and Mark and I had been back at work full time. Sierra received home care from a nurse and then, as her condition progressed and needs lessened; a specialized caregiver looked after her throughout the week. As a family, we had begun to socialize again, regaining our former life to a degree. We had managed to acquire some balance and we were all moving forward.

Now this warped, misshapen part was gouging its way into our lives. I worried that perhaps it was a hernia, thinking that maybe somehow the scar tissue of the repaired diaphragm had ripped and her small intestines were protruding through, but upon closer inspection, the twisted lump was hard and felt like an extension of her ribs.

I cursed myself for letting down my guard and becoming acclimatized to months of manageable stress. On some level, part of me rationalized that if I was always on red alert about her health, I could ward off these obscene physical dangers. Rationally, I knew there was no way one could have foreseen this new wrinkle unfold but I had been in a state of complacency and now a new curve ball blasted my way.

I contacted the head of surgery at Children's explaining what I was seeing, wondering if it could be something to do with the repair of the diaphragm. He felt it was unrelated and recommended I see my local pediatrician. Visiting Kelowna General Hospital as frequently as we did, it was almost as if we had a speed pass to navigate the system. Our pediatrician looked at the lump and felt it was just another part of Sierra's unique anatomy. X-rays were again taken and as the bump grew in size and shape I continued to pursue this new anomaly. Eventually, we were referred to a spinal clinic as they realized that Sierra's spine was twisting vertically and snaking with the added diagnosis of Scoliosis. This protrusion I was seeing was the rib cage twisting towards the front of her body.

In hind sight, it was almost as if we had been given a brief physical and mental rest in the former months in preparation for this new challenge. Reviewing her case with the spinal surgeons at Children's, it was soon confirmed that the bizarre vertical twisting of Sierra's spine was bringing her rib cage around and would eventually squish the lung cavity, restricting her ability to breathe. The news crushed us like an avalanche.

Our visits to Vancouver began again at warp speed. She was seen repeatedly for MRIs and x-rays and eventually she was outfitted for a plastic body brace by a spinal orthotic technician to help slow the rapid twisting of her spine. During these visits, it seemed Sierra's medical team ever increasingly expanded.

Sierra hated her brace. She had to wear a light undershirt beneath the thick hard plastic to keep the brace from brutally chaffing her skin. It restricted her movement and bending capability, just as she had figured out how to run and climb. In the summer it was like a thermal heating vest and I had to ignore the recommendation of her wearing it 23 hours a day to allow her skin some cooling time in the blistering Okanagan heat. The brace had thick velcro straps that tethered the contraption in place and we were to cinch them up tight to restrict the spine from twisting at its alarming rate. As Sierra grew older and more astute, she would hide the brace on us. I once reached in the dryer to get clothes and she had buried it under many shirts in the drum! I had no idea how long she had been without it. On another occasion, I found it hidden behind a bush outside the house as I mowed the lawn.

Summer faded into fall and eventually winter was upon us. It was easier to coerce her into wearing it when it was cold. As we approached Christmas, I mailed out Christmas cards, a feat which had eluded me for several years amidst the chaos. There was one particular person I had kept in touch with throughout the card sending ritual. Ryan's mom, Melody, and I had kept in contact after meeting at Children's and having both children coping with the atrocities of the same affliction.

Ryan's progress really was a beacon of hope for us and I cherished hearing about his growth. The last card had shown a smiling two year old with glasses. His oxygen tube was barely visible and he now had a younger brother with reddish hair.

I excitedly opened the Christmas card once I recognized Melody's name, but it was if I had been sliced through with a sword. Pain and disbelief buffeted me as I took in a picture with only Melody, her husband and their youngest child. I began to read the letter on crisp Christmas paper and began to weep and weep.

Ryan had died.

In the spring, despite his amazing progress medically and his learning to do sign language and play, he had developed a respiratory infection which hospitalized him. Hospitalization for children with diaphragmatic hernia occurs so frequently, parents soon learn to take it as just another blip on the road of life, but Ryan soon digressed into frightening territory. His struggle with his respiratory needs put extra stress on his heart and he went into cardiac arrest twice. He battled on gallantly for several more weeks, but he finally slipped from their grasp in June.

My entire body shook as I read the letter. I weakly carried it out to Mark who was in his workshop across the driveway, and he glanced alarmingly at me when he saw my state.

I just handed him the letter, unable to speak.

In Victoria, in the dark one summer night, I remember Trevor's hands encircling my waist from behind as he gripped to carry me over sharp rocks on the jagged path. I laughed and giggled as I let him lift me to a gentler surface on the far side. I was fifteen and he was sixteen and he was my boyfriend's best friend. Trevor had piercing eyes and a playful soul and I was always at comfortable ease in his presence.

On a sunny Monday morning, a dark force swirled through the dank school hallways. Hush whispers and blank stares engulfed me as I entered the building. My friend relayed the devastating words.

"Trevor is dead."

That solid lump grew heavier in my abdomen.

He had been driving home after work late one Sunday evening and had been extinguished in a lightning quick head on collision. The grade twelve class floated in disbelief above the polished stone floor, shock not allowing their feet to move. My boyfriend and I had broken up months before, but I realized how devastated he would be, so my friends and I decided to leave the school and find him. I knocked many times on his door and finally an empty body opened the entrance, staring blankly at me.

I hugged him asking, "What happened?" He only had the strength to move his shoulders in response.

Trevor's funeral was held above Elk Lake at a church on a mountain peak. The view of the ocean and islands was surreal as hundreds of students gathered to pay our baffled respects. My best friend and I sat side by side, close to the front on the wooden pew. Music from Robert Plant played softly as everyone quietly assembled.

I remember, "*Dancing on My Own*" playing and I scoffed at the irony of the line, "*And I don't care if I die*" as it rang out through the rafters.

Trevor was life ~ daring, risk taking, laughing energy, and now he was gone. Jeanette's hand gripped mine tightly as we endured the service. I held on just as tightly. As we filed out to leave, we each met with the family waiting in reception. I was awed by the calm resignation his parents resonated as they showed more concern for our pain than their own.

Sierra's spinal issues progressed into a nightmare. As she grew, the twist and curve were clearly visible in her stance, yet, in true Sierra fashion, she found ways to adapt and cope with the worsening challenge. She found ways to run in a straight line by leading with her right shoulder.

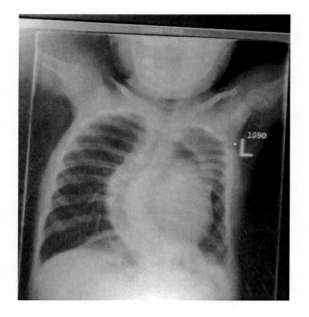

Sierra's spinal x-ray before intervention.

Daniel was also trying to cope with the seriousness of this new condition. At dinner one night, eating a roast chicken, Daniel began identifying the bird's vertebrae and the ribcage and said that if we twisted it, that would be Sierra's spine. I complimented him on his knowledge of the physiology of his sister, but the visual truth dug at me like a butcher knife. I ate little dinner.

Mark hurried to load the truck with his tools and materials for the day. I had already headed in to work and Mark was getting ready to take Daniel and Sierra to daycare and school. Daniel had just started kindergarten and Sierra was walking confidently on pudgy legs. Mark closed the tailgate at the top of the driveway in time to hear Daniel holler from the house.

"Daddy, come quick! Sierra pulled out her tummy tube."

Mark shook his head and rushed down the gravel drive, jumping the stairs to the front door. As he entered the room he saw Daniel dutifully hovering over Sierra, his finger plugging the hole on her stomach where the liquid slowly seeped out.

"Good work, little man." Mark commented as he moved into the back hall to get the spare mic-key kit to replace the burst balloon and tubing.

Daniel kneeled, talking calmly to Sierra, keeping his hand gently but firmly in place. He had seen Mark and I replace this many times and at 5 he could be certified with his First Aid ticket.

Mark unpacked the mic-key material and traded positions with Daniel, telling him to go get the large syringe from the cupboard in her room. Daniel returned, complete with the bottle of sterilized water and the 10 mL syringe. Mark inserted the plastic tubing and balloon into Sierra's weeping hole.

Small amounts of her stomach contents oozed around the plastic as he threaded the tubing through her tight abdominal skin. He took the syringe from Daniel saying, "Good man," again. Mark carefully filled the syringe with the water to inflate the small balloon. Sierra lay still, unflustered as yet another procedure was performed on her while lying prone.

Mark told Sierra how lucky she was to have such a good doctor on hand and Daniel quietly beamed at the compliment.

Sierra was determined to keep up with her hyperactive brother, climbing up the ladder to the tree house and interior loft. She figured out how to ride a bike with training wheels despite her skewed balance and she invented unique ways to bend and put on clothing, maintaining her determination for independence.

Sierra is a force to be reckoned with. Nurses often commented that Sierra could give them a look at only three months old that could make them back off with a procedure, and knowing my daughter, I don't doubt it. She has a strength that most women strive for their entire lives. She is truth, justice and determination ad infinitum. Her depth of strength has mesmerized some of the brightest medical intellects and she does not ever second guess herself. I am constantly learning from this child and her amazing strength of will, as I struggle to keep up to her remarkable standards.

It was early spring and Sierra, now three, continued to develop mentally and physically. Assessments at Children's Hospital continued with the neonatal follow-up clinic evaluating her closely to monitor any progress after the ECMO treatment. Audiology tested her hearing every six months to detect any deterioration in her ability to differentiate sounds. Like a deep lurking shadow, deafness loomed as a possibility following the ECMO intervention and would continue to stalk her up until the age of eight. As a result, we ensured Sierra became well versed in sign language, her little hands dancing and waving to communicate many needs. As an infant, she easily learned the simplistic signing even before she could say many words.

We all learned the basic signs to communicate important aspects of her day and we enjoyed expanding this repertoire with new movements. Sierra was also making progress with her verbal communication, acquiring the sounds of language before any deafness set in.

Part of her assessments included cardiology, tracking the two septal defects in her heart, but miraculously, these seemed to be closing over naturally with the growth of the muscle tissue. Physiotherapists also assessed her regularly to detect any deficits in coordination or large muscle group development.

Sierra had poor muscle tone and was delayed in areas with eye hand coordination, so we ensured she exercised every day. Mark's expertise in this area was invaluable, for at times when I was tempted to coddle Sierra and carry her, Mark would insist that she do it herself and he ensured me that her body would respond by strengthening and expanding her lung volume.

We often went hiking behind our house, as dappled light flickered through the tall pines. Part of the trek rose steeply up the mountain to a rocky outcrop along a deer path. Sierra was determined to try and keep up with her brother as we travelled and she always persevered on these walks. Mark essentially became her personal trainer, ensuring she attempted challenging inclines regularly to build up her cardio-vascular endurance. Unencumbered with tubes and apparatus besides the rigid back brace, Sierra's physical appearance was the same as any other three year old. No one could have imagined that this was the same child we had said goodbye to, tethered by machinery, in that silent room on day seven.

In late March, despite our best efforts and keeping her home out of the daycare cesspools, Sierra succumbed to a dangerous respiratory infection. RSV had been a bullet we had dodged with regular vacci-nations. Each year, because of the severity of her respiratory issues, Sierra had qualified for an insanely expensive vaccine to help protect her from the RSV virus.

Unfortunately, Sierra contracted the wicked illness and she devel-oped severe respiratory distress and needed to be back on oxygen. We used a nebulizer for her every four hours with steroids and bronchial dilatators and being so sick, Sierra lost any appetite. She refused to eat for five days and dropped dangerously close to 20 pounds.

Terrifying waves of fear coursed through me as I envisioned Sierra repeating Ryan's demise. I rushed with Sierra into the hospital for solace and help. Our pediatrician had warned us of just such an occur-rence and now I was coming to her for advice on how to get nour-ishment into my child. I countered that Sierra had grown beyond the need for the feeding tube and had consistently gained weight over the year eating orally.

It was a harrowing few days as we watched Sierra battle the illness. Eventually, to the relief of everyone, she began to progress. As Sierra regained her health after the virus, she began to eat orally and slowly gained weight. I was vigilant in watching her caloric intake and supple-mented her feeding with protein shakes.

Within weeks she was well on her way to recouping her lost strength, but it was a harsh reminder of the reality we faced. It was imperative to keep Sierra's lungs as healthy and viral free as possible.

Music was my refuge.
I could crawl into the space
between the notes
and curl my back
to the loneliness.

~ Maya Angelou

Chapter 14

During her first year at kindergarten, Sierra was finally scheduled for spinal surgery. Our spinal surgeon debated with his colleagues as to the best form of attack to quell the severe twisting of her spine. Her spine was morphing at an alarming rate and she soon had a 60 degree twist threatening her existence.

I dared death to challenge us again, having once been right on the brink of it stealing her away. I was aghast that fate was trying to destroy this child's chance at life, creating an additional flawed design of growth to destroy what little lung capacity she had. I honestly could not have fathomed any more medical issues that Sierra would have to face after the severity of her beginning, yet this new threat progressed with an equal and opposing force to Sierra's will.

The spinal surgeons soon decided that the best approach to counteract Sierra's spinal issues would be to insert recent technology called Telescopic Steel Growing Rods. She was very young to have these embedded, but there was no other medical choice. The rods would be anchored into upper and lower vertebrae via ¾ inch screws and adjustments to the length of the rods would need to be made every six months. Hearing the news and realizing what she would have to endure, I felt like we had both just been sucker punched. To address her severe spinal issues, Sierra would need to have 12 to 14 more surgeries at a rate of two or three a year.

We took in all of the surgeon's information and readjusted our life expectations accordingly. As a family, we had conquered so much already, Mark and I felt we could manage this as well. The added piece was that Sierra was steadily becoming a more cognizant player in these medical discussions. She would hear the words, "deformity", "severity" and "abnormal" and she would openly question why she wasn't normal. At five, she would tell me that she didn't like people saying things were "wrong" with her and I had to be very vigilant about the wording we used in her presence. In all of our eyes she was beyond astonishing, yet when we spoke of her medically it was always in reference to some deficit. I had to make sure that Sierra knew we thought she was incredible the way she was, and that everyone was in fact astounded with whom she was becoming and what she had accomplished, despite the limited negative vocabulary we all used to discuss her medical issues.

The spinal surgery was scheduled for late October and we were to be at Children's Hospital for five or six days. I was shown the contraption that was going to become a lifeline for my daughter and I absorbed it all quietly. Preparation for the surgery required that Sierra's cranium be outfitted with electrical sensors to monitor the delicate nerve connections throughout the surgery to ensure no nerve damage occurred during surgery. The long steel rods needed to be placed through the posterior muscle tissue and attached into the bone of the vertebrae.

Mark was there for the initial surgery, but he was scheduled to leave as soon as the operation was complete and she was stable. I would stay with Sierra throughout her initial recovery at the hospital, then bring her home to continue her month long rejuvenation.

Sierra would quietly bring up the concept of the surgery and I soon realized she was extremely terrified of being cut open. She often asked me if she might bleed to death while in surgery and I had to reassure her that the doctors and nurses were going to keep her safe and just make a small opening. It was obscene how big the multiple incisions actually proved to be.

The day of her surgery I came down with a severe stomach flu. In the pediatric ward we were fortunate to get a private room with a bathroom, so I was able to care for Sierra then quickly retreat to the washroom to be sick. On day three when a friend came to visit she looked visibly shocked to see how pale I had become. Sierra was bravely suffering much worse.

She was in severe pain and on extremely strong pain killers and morphine. Each time she had to go to the washroom I had to gently carry her and set her down. X-rays showed the operation went well and that the placement of the rods was going to be effective. She could move all of her extremities and the incisions were beginning to heal. Her back had been sliced open in two places and she had a four inch gash at the top and another along her lower back. The staples looked huge against her fiery swollen skin but I was careful not to let the shock show as I first glanced at her back.

Her kindergarten teacher had a dozen red roses delivered to her hospital room in Vancouver with a metallic cat balloon and child life social workers regularly came to bring Sierra quiet activities and books to ensure that some semblance of child play could continue. On the fourth day, Sierra was strong enough for me to wheel her to the central play area and she did an activity with three other children for about ten minutes before becoming exhausted and needing to retire to her bed.

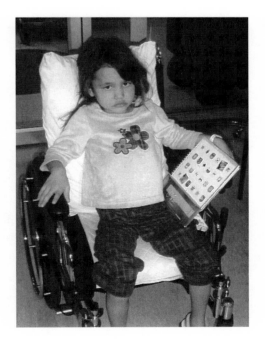

The spinal surgeon had Sierra stand and take a few steps days after the operation and he was confident that Sierra was well on the way to recovery. I was given the instructions for administering the pain medication and shown ways to support Sierra so she could soon regain her mobility. Sierra was released on the fifth day and we began the long trek home in the car with Sierra lying, cushioned in the rear seat. I rigged a way to keep her seat belted while lying prone and gave her the codeine before beginning our rainy trip home.

Sierra rarely complains, but it became obvious how much pain she was in as the medication wore off. Her muscle tissue had been severed to insert the rods and it was difficult for her to move without triggering waves of pain. When we did finally arrive home, her bed became the couch in the living room for the next three weeks, and we carried her carefully to the washroom. She would listen to soothing music on the couch after taking her medication. She was so brave throughout the ordeal and I hated to imaging her having to endure this every six months for the next eight or nine years.

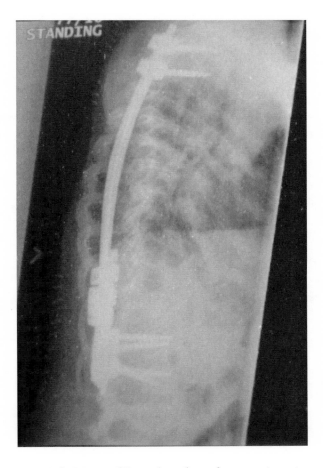

X-ray Side View of Sierra's rods and screws in spine.
Telescopic Growing Rods inserted in Sierra at 5 years.

Days after having her home, I thought I had processed everything and that I was over the worst of the shock, but after meeting a friend one evening and talking about the ordeal, I came home and went for a walk in the woods. I was overcome with grief and softly cried as I allowed myself to envision the metal contraption now wedged with large screws into my child's back. I screamed aloud, cursing God for forcing my child to go through such constant torture, then, I crumpled on the moss covered forest floor and allowed violent sobs to wrack my body until I could cry no more.

Everyone thinks we are so fortunate to have the technology to do what we do, but if each individual were forced to witness the immense pain and confusion these children go through they would understand that it is never just black and white. I would do almost anything to stop the cycle of pain Sierra was now forced to enter over the next decade.

Chapter 15

At first dreams seem impossible,
then improbable,
then inevitable.

~ Christopher Reeves

It always stopped me cold; a new anomaly of Sierra's physiology. By now, I should have known there would never be an end to these hidden hurdles in life, but they crumpled me repeatedly under a heavy avalanche of brutal cognition.

I had tried to avoid seeing it, the lump growing redder and larger around her sinus. But after months of watching it morph and feeling the solidness of the growth on only one side of her nasal cavity, I finally began the pursuit through the ridiculous medical maze. First, the visit to the family doctor for a referral to a local ENT Specialist who makes another referral to Children's for their ENT specialist to look at it, then on to the Genetic Specialists and let's throw in plastic surgery as well for their diagnostic two cents.

We are extremely fortunate to be in Canada and have the medical services we do, but I was now a veteran player in this game and had grown board of the landscape. During one of Sierra's operation recoveries at Children's Hospital, I pushed for Respiratory Therapy to look into the obtrusive growth and explained my observations of her constant nasal drip from the same side. As I delved into the mysteries, I knew I didn't want to find the truth.

Within hours, the ENT specialist, after being contacted by the Respiratory Department, ordered a CAT scan to look into the growth on Sierra's face. Even after all I had witnessed at this hospital, I was flabbergasted when they fast tracked her for the CAT scan that afternoon. Speed is not always a good indication in the medical system. My nervous system immediately went on red alert.

They wheeled her down in her sore condition, just 48 hours after the spinal surgery, this time to delve into the shrouded truth in her skull. That comforting familiar calm settled over my whole being once again as I focused on coaxing Sierra to not be frightened of the looming "donut" machine. She was heavily sedated and strapped snuggly onto the board to be slid gently into the monolith.

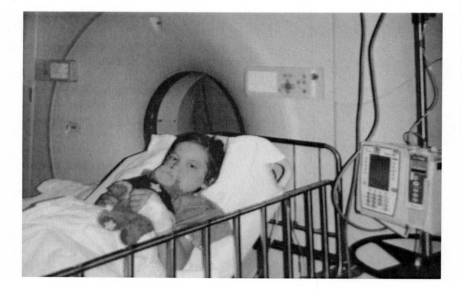

The following day, I met with the Ear Nose and Throat specialist who thankfully ruled out a malignant cancerous growth. There was still puzzlement as to what was causing the increased bone growth in just the left nasal cavity and surrounding facial bone, but it was minimally impeding her respiratory function. I silently wondered how anything else could impede this small creature's respiratory function … what was left to go wrong?!

In the months to follow we would be seen by geneticists who also were confused by the abnormal bone growth Sierra was presenting. I had to use all of my will power not be rude as they inquired, *for educational purposes,* into Sierra's medical history and into our genetic background for clues for their file. I knew little would come from our meeting which would aid Sierra.

After all the various fields involved in the diagnostic tests had collaborated and conferred, they concluded that this was just another unique feature of Sierra's anatomy and agreed to continue to monitor it for any further developments. Meanwhile, each day I glanced at this red lump praying the advanced bone growth was only growing outward and not inward as well, blocking her nasal airway.

In fairness, children with moderate to severe Congenital Diaphragmatic Hernia rarely survived until just fifteen years ago. The ECMO technology and other respiratory advances have allowed the existence of many children who just a few years ago would not have survived. No one knows the prolonged outcome for these children, but with that uncertainty also comes a brilliant hope, precisely because no one does know the prolonged outcome.

Positive, pure vision has had a major impact on Sierra's development. We refused to believe any other path. We envisioned our daughter as strong, smart, capable and physically able and we witnessed the ramifications of that vision each day.

Life is sorrow, overcome it.
Life is a song, sing it.

~ Mother Theresa

Chapter 16

"I don't want to go, Mommy!" Sierra's green flecked eyes brimmed with silky tears, pleading with mine for some sanctuary. Sierra was now eight years old facing her eighth operation.

Both she and I knew there was no way to avoid the inevitable, but we lurched forward awkwardly, moved by the painful truth.

"This is something that has to happen, honey. I would stop it if I could, but you need this operation." My attempt at a feeble explanation spilled forth unconvincingly.

Anger and fear shrouded her gentle face. I was awed by her courage. Finally, after a strained silence, she spoke. "The parts I hate the most are the needles, the pain in my back and when they tear off the bandage."

It was the first time she ever really vocalized her fear and I stopped to listen intently. She was still so young and had already endured so much pain.

I flashed back to a summer afternoon on the linoleum floor in our kitchen in Edmonton as my six year old self yelped and carried on while my mother tried to remove a splinter from my finger. She would attempt to ease it out of my soft flesh with a sterile needle she had swung to and fro through the flame of a match, blackening the tip. I would twist and flail as she tried to touch the festered skin around the tiny wound. To me, the needle represented a horror of pain that in fact was no more than a gentle, minute pressure, but to my childish, inflamed imagination, I saw the needle digging savagely into my skin, invoking pain too hot to endure. This scene gravely paled in comparison to what Sierra endured with disturbing frequency.

I looked at Sierra now, salty tears streaked her soft creamy skin. I could only imagine the courage it took to face the fear of these operations, so beyond her control. In her eyes I could see a flash of anger as she fumed at the injustice of it all. I reached to hug her, trying to will her pain and fear deep into my body. To see her like this ripped at my soul.

In the hospital room preparing for surgery, two nurses came through the drapes, telling Sierra they were there to "draw on her head." I smiled softly as I watched their polished bedside manner.

"We are going to draw little shapes in your hair, just like this." The nurse said as she drew a red heart lightly on Sierra's hand and Sierra smiled. "Is that okay?"

Sierra nodded in approval and flashed me a quizzical look. The two nurses in the colourful bandanas began to take precise measurements of Sierra's skull for the EEG sensors that would monitor her brain activity throughout the spinal operation. Red and blue marks were strategically etched on her scalp. Another nurse entered with medications and swabs saying that the blood work would soon be taken.

Sierra sat, fussed over like a child bride, as she was prepped for the looming surgery. I stroked her arm whenever I could to try and provide some hint of reassurance. I felt myself slowly morphing into my stronger peaceful state as the pace of entering technicians and anesthesiologists began to increase.

I could sense this transformation now. It was a deep strength that rose silently and observed the scene, causing any fear to dissipate. It becomes a union with my peaceful consciousness and space and time dissolve. I cannot yet will myself into this state, but it flows through me at times like these when I need unlimited strength and courage.

After initial assessments and x-rays, the medical team began wheeling Sierra down the hall toward the big, metal doors and I walked along side holding her hand, making an effort to maintain a casual, measured banter with the anesthetist as we approached the sterile surgical bay.

Familiar beeps and ten faces greeted us in the OR, each person intently immersed in their role. Sierra finally let her tears fall. She looked at me, eyes begging to pick her up and run, but I gazed peacefully, lovingly back saying, "It is going to be all right. I am right here."

I could not let my mind move to the reality of the next few hours, knowing that on some level Sierra would sense my fear. Medically, I understood the procedure, but as a parent, I could not allow myself to envision the graphic nature of what would really happen in this room.

Nurses quickly layed sensors on Sierra's bare chest and the cardiac and respiratory monitors flashed to life. The plastic light sensors were attached to her finger to monitor her blood oxygen level. The rhythm of all ten bodies increased in synched movement as the oxygen mask was placed over her face. Sierra panicked and became upset and finally, they induced her forced slumber through the IV needle and I watched as her body rapidly went limp, her head falling abnormally to the side. That was when I was quickly whisked away, to ensure I did not witness the procedure.

I wished just once I could stay to get a true glimpse of the inside of my daughter. Such mysteries lay veiled beneath her golden skin.

I knew they would have her prone, on her front, wedged in the bizarre contraption I had seen in the OR. Her neck would be in a brace of sorts. She would be intubated and on a ventilator, mechanical breaths yet again inflating her tiny chest. Sensors of vibrant colours would lead lines from her skull to the EEG. Other electrical sensors would trace the tangled waves across her delicate chest.

Her back, with little railroad tracks on top and bottom, scars from previous surgeries, would be smeared with sterile orange antiseptic solution that would take days to scrub off. Her orthotic surgeon, who we had spoken with early that morning, would look intently at the most recent X-rays and determine the first point of entry.

Months ago, we were told there was a problem with the spinal correction. The growing rods were not providing sufficient torque to correct the alarming twisting of Sierra's spine. The rib cage continued to twist forward, threatening to decrease the area where her right lung could expand. This operation would be an attempt to re-anchor the highest set of clamps, re-drilling into Sierra's tiny vertebrae, adding more screws further down the spinal column, to pull the rib cage back the other way. More sharp metal would be embedded into Sierra's living bone.

First the medical team would carefully slice into her tender back, the scalpel making a slick incision through the epidermis and dermis. Rich, scarlet blood would trickle, following the symmetrical ridges of scar tissue left by previous staples; some of it would pool in those man-made dimples. A symphony of constant beeping and singing of machinery would be the sonata for my daughter's vital signs as she lay limp and unresponsive beneath thin blue sheets.

In my mind, I could see it all ... but they would not let me stay.

Chapter 17

Luminous beings are we,
not this crude matter.
You must feel the Force around you;
between you and me, the tree, the rock,
everywhere.

Yoda — George Lucas

Their beautiful silhouettes cast long shadows on our sloping expanse of lawn. Stubborn determination, lightning quick humour, strong musculature on sinewy bodies grace both my children as they run through the sprinkler as twilight descends. Their beautiful, unique bloodline is woven so tightly with many different hues; Irish, First Nation, Jamaican, Spanish and Scottish. Their spiritedness is not for the faint of heart.

They bicker and quarrel as siblings, then roll in wicked waves of laughter at a shared joke, merging as one. The love they share grows deeper beneath the murky childhood stream of jealousy and sibling rivalry.

In rare moments, when I force myself to be still, I listen to their giggles, discussions and plans which soon erupt into disdain and tumultuous clamor.

It is at these moments I smile, cherishing their gift, seeing their healthy spontaneity being free and wild on the grass against the setting sun.

When my grandmother died, I felt I had lost a great anchor. A guide who knew the way was quietly extinguished and gone, all of her knowledge dissipating into the ether. It was several months before our extended family could make the trip to Jamaica to return her ashes to their rightful resting place, situated beside her husband and first born daughter in a graveyard in Kingston.

My children had never been to Jamaica. They had never travelled outside of Canada and it was a trip that revealed many harsh truths of our world. Jamaica is an enigma of incredible wealth and opulence, a reward for the selfish, corrupt few, and a desolate, dilapidated system of gradual decay that was shamefully run into the ground by ego driven aristocrats. The natural beauty is hellishly scarred by internationally acclaimed, luxury hotels; false monuments of greed and wealth, while across the street from their grand, glittering entrances, shanty towns are hinged together with cardboard and corrugated metal; shelter to human beings with pure hearts and real dreams.

I had not been to Jamaica for fifteen years. As a child, I was incredibly fortunate to travel to Jamaica almost yearly. I was christened there, celebrated my first birthday with my Jamaican cousins, and returned almost every Christmas to vacation in my grandmother's cottage in Ocho Rios, spending countless hours building castles on the white sand beaches and catching hermit crabs and geckos with my sister. I got to experience true Jamaican culture as I visited aunts, uncles and cousins in various towns across the island. Jamaicans are a loving people who cherish the purity of childhood and the strong bonds of family. We were always welcomed with smiles and open arms and we were fully engulfed into Jamaican life and celebrations.

I loved going to the market, small shelters set up side by side displaying fruit, ceramics, crafts and clothing. The colours and fragrances of the market were surreal, lifting our small bodies forward to each new curiousity. There was a tangible gaiety and excitement within the market as playful bartering tumbled from ebony faces with wide ivory smiles. My father, white as any Scot born in Winnipeg, would be lobster red from the sun, but he loved to venture through the markets and side roads to investigate the towns. My father has an insatiable desire to explore which I found exciting and invigorating as a young child. He would walk anywhere for hours and he was so personable, he could strike up pleasant conversation with anyone.

In the late 1970s, Jamaica was still a very safe island to explore and many beaches were still bereft of monstrous hotel chains. It was pristine and I cherished each gift of time we had during the winter.

Now, in 2008, Jamaica had sadly transformed into a corrupt, crumbling economy fed by greed. Many Jamaicans struggled for their daily existence as the value of their dollar continued to fall to ridiculous lows. As we drove through Kingston, my children's eyes took in the poverty and struggle of a nation my grandmother and Mom had spoken of so proudly. Daniel and Sierra had never seen human beings living in cardboard and metal shacks, walking in ripped clothing. There were also expensive vehicles and large houses in the mountains to glare in stark contrast to the paucity.

The morning of my Grandmother's memorial service, I helped my children dress and we walked quietly to the area in Phyllis's house where she had prepared a traditional breakfast. Phyllis was a lifelong friend of my Grandmother and Mom and she lived in a large home in Kingston, but for protection, the windows had bars and the doors had barred gates. The hallway to the bedrooms also had a barred gate that she would ensure was locked tight at night. I remembered this from staying there as a child, for it had terrified me as it would clang shut, reverberation signally our caged existence through the concrete hallway.

In the mid morning sun, we arrived at the Anglican Church, peeling our legs off the seats of the car in the stifling July humidity. This was the same church my sister and I had been baptized in as infants donning filmy satin gowns. Now, our cotton clothes clung to our sticky skin and we continuously wiped our brows. Distant relatives and friends greeted us warmly, recognizing my sister and me from when we were children. I recognized only a fraction of the faces, but they all draped us in sincerity and affection. I had to smile as my sister's children and mine began to play hide and seek amongst the granite gravestones as they waited for the service to begin. Children will find joy and play in any environment and it lightened my heart to watch them laugh in the dappled tropical light.

After the service and laying my Grandmother's ashes to rest, we made the long trek to the other side of the island in a van with 15 members of our family. My sister's family, my cousin's family, my son and daughter and my Mom all crammed into the small vehicle for the four hour drive over the precarious winding mountain road.

In true North American fashion, we spent the last four days of our stay in Jamaica in one of the opulent hotels I have grown to despise. I would lie if I said we didn't enjoy ourselves, but the disparity that existed within hundreds of feet of that facility almost made me physically ill.

One morning, as the large group of us took our small children for a walk along the white sand beach, we passed a woman beneath a tarp in the trees who was braiding tourists' hair and selling small trinkets. About thirty feet from her, a five year old girl with beautiful ebony skin splashed in the water and called up to the woman to watch her latest game. The woman braiding the hair looked up and smiled, revealing missing teeth, but her face shone brilliantly with love and pride as she gazed at her daughter. I stood silently as the purity and simplicity of the moment spread through my soul.

The night before, my sister, a Crown Prosecutor, my cousin's wife, a Dentist and Professor at Stanford and I, a special educator had wallowed in our shared stories of stressfully trying to balance motherhood and demanding careers. We complained of all of the unique experiences we were missing with our children who ranged in age from two to eight. We lamented on how ridiculous the struggle was to keep up the false expectations of society to have a new car, a large, landscaped home and vacations in tropical locations.

Now here I gazed at a woman who had very little, but spent her days on a sandy beach while her daughter spent all day playing in the warm, salty surf. Instantly I knew who the more fortunate individual was. Now, I just had to gain the strength to let go of my false beliefs.

It would be several years and many spinal operations later until my world ground to a stagnant halt, forcing me to change my trajectory for good.

There are only two mistakes
one can make along the road to truth;
not searching all the way,
and not starting.

~ Buddha

Chapter 18

My body gently sways, wrapped firmly in blankets and belted tightly to the stretcher. A paramedic hovers over me asking for shreds of medical details then he flicks off the harsh lighting as the ambulance begins to move. I lay silent, shrouded in the dim light of the breaking dawn eerily glowing through the small rear window.

It is an icy November morning and my skin is unusually cold as the vehicle travels south across the Okanagan mountain road. As we arrive at the hospital, the paramedics gently unload me and wheel me through the mechanical doors, down the twisting corridors to the crowded catheter lab.

A kind nurse preps me for the angiogram and soon I am wheeled into a busy room. A large camera hangs suspended on a beige hydraulic arm. Four large black monitors light up with dazzling images; spectrums of colour assault my eyes.

The doctor expertly threads the specialized catheter through my femoral artery, moving carefully up to my heart. As the tube loops on the screen, I watch awestruck as the radioisotope is released and my coronary arteries emerge as vivid apparitions on the grey scale screen. Beautiful, twisting branches appear in gentle French curves, reminiscent of the vines of a delicate wild rose.

I watch again and again as the brief clip is displayed. "The coronary arteries look clear," the doctor states confidently, allowing me to relax my clenched fists. Another negative test result, but the inquiry remains. What is the real issue for the constriction in my chest?

Days before at work, stress mounted in waves. It was a normal condition which I fooled myself into believing was essential to maintain my drive. At the age of 39, thinking I had learned so much from experience, I still placed myself under the impossible demands of work, parenthood, perfectionism and ignored my health.

I was now an administrator, and I still supported many students with special needs. Sierra still needed to have her spinal surgeries every six months, which required up to a week at the hospital to recover. Daniel was on the verge of becoming a teenager with his own demands. I was gradually becoming more and more consumed and tired, but attributed it to the demands of a new job. Each night I would go to bed earlier and earlier, sometimes not even wanting to eat.

My weekends were spent catching up on work, squeezing in time with my children and sleeping to face the following week's demands. Often, I would feel my heart racing and occasionally I would be winded just climbing the stairs.

In the three years leading up to this time I had completed several triathlons. I had been running in the summer and swimming up to a mile four times a week before I began my new job. Since the position commenced, I had not exercised once. I still felt healthy, so the morning when I first felt the crushing pressure on my chest, I attributed it to indigestion. After an hour of the pain coming and going, but increasing in pressure, I decided to go sit quietly in my office to see if it would pass.

On my way down the long hall, a jagged, splintering pain ripped through my chest and I had to gasp for breath. I felt like I was going to pass out, and couldn't get enough air. I was driven to the hospital and quickly admitted, placed in the emergency trauma ward.

The EKG was showing inverted T waves and bradycardiac rhythms. I was given oxygen, beta-blockers, nitrous spray and I was soon seen by a cardiologist. He thought at first it was just a sign of stress and anxiety, but after being admitted to the ICU Cardiac Ward, days later I had an Echocardiogram. I knew this technology well from experiences with Sierra and I could almost sense when the technician located the anomaly.

Days later I learned that I did have an internal issue with my heart. There was an obstruction in the Aortic Valve. A sub-aortic membrane was impeding some blood flow from the ventricle out the aortic artery, but it alone was not enough to be causing the crushing chest pains. The cause of my affliction was still a mystery.

When Daniel came into the hospital room the second day, he clung to me for many minutes, hiding his face from mine. He would not release his grip, and I felt fear course through his clenched, sinuous muscles. I suddenly realized I was at a crossroads and needed to make some serious decisions. I needed to find the courage to give up my false illusion of comfort. My children's needs trumped any professional ambition.

The mystery of life
is not a problem to be solved
but a reality to be experienced.

~ Art Van Der Leeuw

Chapter 19

Sierra smiles as she carefully films the lump now beginning to move on shore, lumbering its great weight toward the sea. It breathes deeply a moment before taking the last few strenuous pulls toward the ocean. The giant sea turtle glistens as her massive shell is engulfed by the surf. She swims toward me with graceful strength, peering at me closely for a brief moment, before changing course. Yellow green eyes gaze deeply into mine before she propels away across the reef.

"That was amazing!" I sputter as I wrestle with my snorkel gear, wading up to the Na Pali shoreline. Solid red, grey cliffs rise above us just beyond the golden sand. Turquoise waves crash into each other with playful vengeance meters beyond as sunlight flickers pristinely off the crests.

"Mommy, I got it! I got it!" Sierra sparkles with joy as she runs to show me the footage of the sea turtle leaving the shore. "I filmed her all the way from the rocks to the ocean!"

She is so excited to be immersed in this tropical wonderland. I watch as she carefully negotiates the volcanic rocks up to the path at the tree line. Her long hair blows freely in the breeze, brushing her spine with a soft caress.

The letter waits silently in the dark metal box at home. The next surgery will be in two weeks, but for now, ignorance and play envelope our worlds as we are entranced by the beauty of the pristine Na Pali coast and quietly observe the magic of its existence.

Five years before, an amazing colleague, mentor and friend had died quickly of pancreatic cancer. At the time of her diagnosis, she was editing my thesis and giving me the encouragement to complete the work. When we discovered her fate and she quickly slipped from our grasp, my reality was rocked with a fierce, unsettling sense of brevity and the concept of object impermanence spiraled into a helix of mass confusion.

Those weeks immediately following her death, my energy and thoughts were in chaos. One morning, I lost partial vision out of one eye for over an hour and the doctors checked me for stroke. This entire, unsettling experience became a portal into my creative energy; murky and frightening, but there.

I had a dream about Ailsa days after she died. It has been of great comfort to me and I come back to reflect on it often during my day to regain composure and perspective, or simply, to allow me to see the humour and joy of life.

In the dream, I was in a strange house — the typical split level floor plan of so many North American homes. The house was mine and many people were over. I was running around the harshly lit basement, chasing my children, trying to get them to put their pajamas on for bed. They were playing tag, laughing and enjoying the game, not listening to my requests. The doorbell rang, so I ran up the half-flight of stairs and opened the door, and there was Ailsa, elegant as always, wanting to visit.

I led her downstairs feeling tremendous dread as she saw my children running rampant, people everywhere in my home and the house in disarray. I took her into a side room, thinking it would be a quieter, less hectic place to talk, only to see a wall of water pouring down where an exposed plumbing pipe had burst. Water was pouring everywhere and my children were still running around, giggling wildly. I felt as if I had no control and was deeply embarrassed. Ailsa looked at the water, the kids, then at me and started laughing, her beautiful eyes sparkling mischievously. I awoke to this one thought.

"Chaos is the meaning."

It was as if Ailsa was trying to let me know that this is the meaning of life — this chaotic, nonsensical, scrambled mess — and that was the beauty and perfection of it all. She was telling me to stop trying to control it and enjoy it all; every messy, crazy, tumultuous step of the way.

I especially treasure the fact that it was a wall of water. I have a deep affinity for water and waterfalls. There seemed no beauty to me during the dream as water gushed down the unfinished cement wall, but it did sparkle and splash — as any waterfall does.

Will these words serve a purpose? I feel I am supposed to record these thoughts, for others to read at some point, but to me tonight they seem a rambling, mangled, disjointed mess.

Chaos.

And we are all intertwined...

Epilogue

"Explicitus est liber."
'The scroll is unrolled.'

Sierra continues to make incredible progress and her story has mysti-fied and inspired many. She is intelligent, strong, active and full of life. However, the spinal operations continue to surface with consistent regularity, like a sad chorus in a song that must be repeated.

We owe so much to the medical professionals in every discipline at both facilities who have enabled Sierra to survive. While we may not have seen eye to eye on every decision, their knowledge, patience and devotion have been invaluable. They are all a credit to their profession and we are grateful for their commitment and tireless effort.

At the time of the initial diagnosis, we were told Sierra would have less than a 25% chance of survival. There was very little information that was easily accessible concerning Congenital Diaphragmatic Hernia, and as demonstrated, each case can be so different in severity and treatment. Parents who may be experiencing this trauma or some-thing similar should have faith in two things:

We never know what treasures
life has in store.

You have a depth of unlimited strength
deep within.

Sierra and Michelle

When I let go of what I am,
I become what I might be.

~ Loa Tzu